Unified Bulwarked Etherveil Canister for Coadjutant Ransack

Modesta

Unified Bulwarked Etherveil Canister for Coadjutant Ransack

First Edition September 2025

Written by Modesta

TABLE OF CONTENTS

TABLE OF CONTENTS

CHAPTER 1

CHAPTER 1

INTRODUCTION

1.1 Preface

This chapter presents the proposed research work concisely, which strives for the design of a cloud computing based collaborative research frame work with enhanced security and access control. This chapter explains study background, determined research problems, motivation, objectives, research methodology, and thesis organization.

1.2 Background

This section discusses about the concepts that serves as the foundation for this thesis.

1.2.1 Collaborative Research

Inter institutional and intra institutional collaborations are imperatives in the field of complex, expensive and ingenious scientific research. The multi-dimensional nature of scientific research often demands collaboration between individuals or institutions. Scientific research collaborations involve researchers from several institutions who collaborate to share data or analysis tools based on their research requisites [54]. Collaborative research contributes to the research communities in innumerable ways, with validation and verification of results, abets further inventive analysis on datasets derived from experiments and also lowering of costs by avoiding repetition of data collection. Scientist from various research fields have agreed upon the need to collaborate and share the resources to deal with challenges in massive data acquisition and processing power.

1.2.2 Scope & Opportunity

Collaborations are indispensable in interdisciplinary and multidisciplinary research, which requires pooling of knowledge and ideas, develop procedures. exchange data and tools to facilitate sophisticated problem solving. The up surging intricacy of research, in disciplines that requires specialized resources and expertise are significantly benefitted through collaboration [51]. Collaborations has attained greater significance in diverse research fields like biomedical engineering, astrophysics, health informatics, Big data analytics, Nano technology, etc. as it significantly reduces the cost and effort in carrying out the research, expedite the research outcome with improved reliability.

1.2.3 Research Significance

The advent of ICT, Open standards, Open source software, internet and World Wide Web and advancement in web technologies have prominently boosted the collaborative efforts in scientific research. Sharing of data, analysis tools or results are vital for scientific research collaborations. Even if many file storage services and content management solutions are existing, it is unfeasible to use these services for enormously sized research data. Latterly, Virtual Research Environments (VRE), Science Clouds have substituted domain specific and confined conventional grid or cluster based e-infrastructures. However, concerns exist about the confidentiality and privacy of sensitive research data and resources in collaborative environments. Most of the existing platforms for collaborative research, deploy customary access control mechanisms that are role specific, and the original research owner does not have control over the shared resources beyond the policy enforcement points [65]. Researchers may require to recreate computational environments in order to produce results changing the parameters [33]. The collaborative research frameworks ought to enable researchers from different organisations to collaborate and facilitate to analyse the data available in any repository using a tool available anywhere [43]. Thus reproducibility, heterogeneity and flexibility are very essential features for a collaborative research platform. Most of the existing frameworks for scientific or academic research lacks the above said features. Hence it is significant to investigate collaborative research to resolve the above said problems.

1.2.4 Cloud Computing

Cloud computing, like earlier computing paradigms cluster, grid, have intended at providing computing as a utility. Cloud computing is an internet based service delivery model, built on virtualization, that offers software infrastructure, platform and other computing resources to the users on" pay –as you go" basis. The services are availed from third party service provider as a metered utility while the customer concentrates on his primary business without possessing any physical infrastructure. The service providers deploy the services through internet and consumers can access the service anywhere anytime.

NIST (National Institute of standards and technology) has defined Cloud Computing as "A model for enabling ubiquitous, convenient, on-demand network access to a shared pool of configurable computing resources (e.g., networks, servers, storage, applications, and services) that can be rapidly provisioned and released with minimal management effort or service provider interaction" [63]. The model consists of five important characteristics, three service models, and four deployment models. The types of services that a business can provide using cloud computing are called service models and the nature and scope of the cloud is termed as the deployment models.

Cloud derives its features from many other earlier computing sirens like cluster, grid etc., The on-demand self-service aspect of cloud computing provide the user access to any service anytime, anywhere. User provision the resources such as storage, bandwidth or processing directly and is devoid of any interfacing with the service provider. The resources such as compute, storage, memory that are pooled can be dynamically allocated based on the consumer's requirements. Numerous users share the physical and virtual resources from various data centres without being apprehensive about the location or origin of the resources. This location independence feature of cloud computing is attained through multitenancy. Multitenancy is a type of computing architecture in which single instance of an application runs on multiple client machines called as tenants. Multiple virtual instances of the resources are made available for the multiple users in a multitenant architecture through virtualization technology. The scalability of cloud services empowers the users to acquire and pay for resources according to the demand. The elastic provisioning of resources enables the applications to demand resources according to the varying workload and release it back when not in use. Cloud systems powers on metering capability to control and monitor and by this means optimize the resource usage. The metering system provides transparency to the service provider as well the user regarding the utilized resources. The resources are accessible through different devices, everywhere over the network which promotes heterogeneity.

NIST has recognized four standard cloud deployment models which are public cloud, private cloud, community cloud, and hybrid cloud. These depict a particular form of cloud infrastructure differentiated by means of scope, ownership and access. The service provider deploys a public cloud system for public access and exists. The services are available for the public over internet which users access through web browsers. public cloud offers high scalability, location independence and are cost efficient. A private cloud is put up on a private network and accessed by internal users of a single organisation. Private clouds are expensive than public clouds, but it renders better reliability, privacy and security. In case of a sudden rise in demand for resources, private clouds apply cloud bursting. A community cloud is provisioned for confined usage of specialized community of users from organizations that has related requirements. Community cloud allows for increased customization than publically hosted cloud. Hybrid cloud is a flexible deployment model which is combines the features of public clouds and private clouds.

The common cloud service models are Software as a Service (SaaS), Platform as a Service (PaaS), Infrastructure as a Service (IaaS). Software as a Service (SaaS) model enables the customer access to the service provider's software and applications using web browsers or API through Internet. Platform as a Service (PaaS) aids users to develop and deliver applications using the cloud based platform offered by the service provider. The entire environment is maintained by the service provider. Infrastructure as a Service (IaaS) providers make available processing, storage, networks and other essential computing resources and user can run any software together with operating systems and applications. Thus the user is offered a platform virtualization environment with storage and networking.

1.2.5 Overview of Virtualization Techniques

Virtualization is the method of building virtual instances of the resources called as Virtual Machine (VM) and separate them to many implementation environments. IT organisations has widely embraced virtualization technology to take in autonomic computing that facilitate fine grained resource management and dynamic resource allocation. Some of the primary benefits of virtualisation are physical hardware independence, multitenancy, elasticity, enhanced isolation, and improved security.

The various types of virtualization techniques employed in cloud computing are summarized below:

Server virtualization generates virtual instances that operates like physical server, isolated from each other. with adequate abstraction for the server resources. Network virtualization splits up the usable bandwidth, to distinct secured channels, from the available set of system resources and are allotted to any device. Storage virtualization pools physical storage from numerous devices to a single storage. Full virtualization offers isolation to operating systems and applications by means of hypervisor and brings in abstraction for each Virtual Machine.

In Para virtualization, hypervisor alters the guest operating system. Operating System level virtualization or container-based virtualization generates isolated user instances. Though hypervisor-based virtualization provides satisfactory isolation among guest virtual machines, it has heavy overheads. Container-based virtualization, virtualizes the host operating and enable several guest containers to ride above the host operating system, not requiring to mount extra kernel for the guest containers, which significantly reduces the performance overhead.

KVM (Kernel-based Virtual Machine)

KVM is a hypervisor-based virtualization approach for Linux that comprises of a Virtual Machine Monitor (VMM) upon the host operating system. KVM follows full virtualization through installation of an unaltered guest operating system (OS) for Linux process. It offers extremely sound isolation though it incurs more overheads and wastage of storage space.

LXC (Linux containers)

Container-based virtualization or Operating System Level virtualization offers a lightweight substitute in comparison to hypervisors. LXC play a pivot role in Containerization technology. Kernel namespaces and control groups achieve the light weight isolation among guests and host operating system in Linux kernels. While namespaces offer resource and network isolation, cgroups bring about management of the resources, process control and the network configuration. LXC make use of Linux Kernel features like chroot, PID to enable users to build and manage applications by means of APIs.

Docker

Docker platform follows lightweight virtualization technology and is based on LXC. The containerized application and corresponding dependencies incurs less overhead compared to a VM. This Linux based open platform expedites fast development and execution of applications, together with a set of tools and workflows for effortless deployment and management.

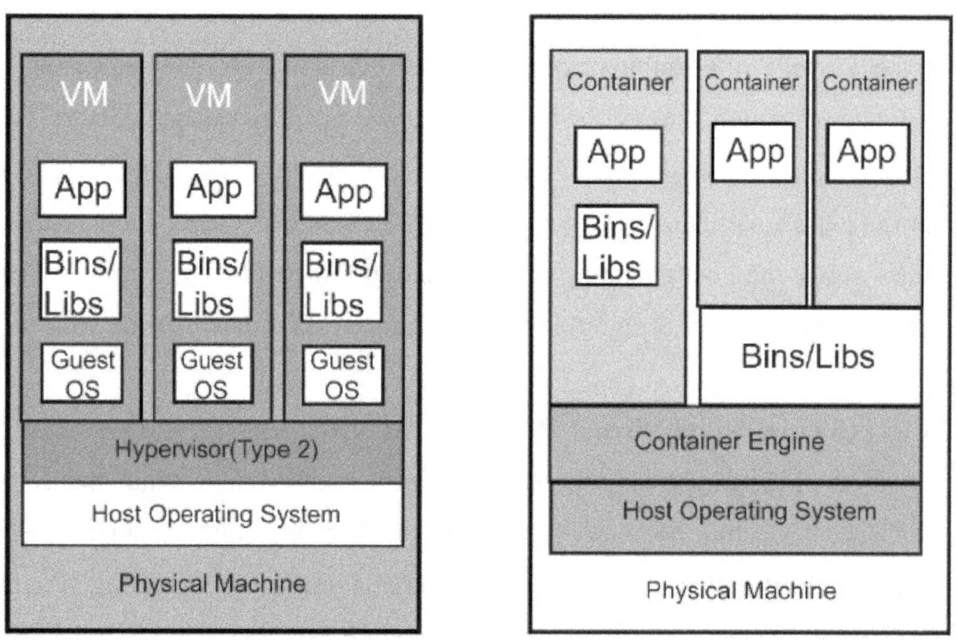

Figure 1. 1 : Container-based and Hypervisor-based Virtualization

1.2.6 Overview of Access Control Methods

Authentication and authorisation of users is a significant concern in a multiuser environment. Various security problems that arise in multitenant cloud environments can be resolved through strong access control mechanisms. Some of those access control methods generally used in cloud systems are discussed below:

Discretionary Access Control (DAC)

DAC method allows the resource owner to assign the access privileges for the users and limits the right to use of resource as per the user's identity. Access Control List (ACL) defines access control privileges for every user. The administrator applies these access policies to the files and directories. DAC is the built in access control technique used in UNIX systems where security attributes are applied to the subjects. The user decides the access privileges to objects and rights are set accordingly.

Role Based Access Control (RBAC)

In this access control technique, access to the resources are established depending on the role of the subject in an organization. Read, Write, Execute rights of a user on the container objects is role specific. The user can carry out operations on the objects based on the rights given. Due to inefficiency of ACL in cloud systems with vast number of users, hybrid approaches with RBAC and ACL are implemented, aimed at secured authorization. DAC and RBAC implement the access control constraints by way of the application interfaces. However, such access control checks are easily escaped in web based systems, is a major shortfall of these models.

Mandatory Access Control (MAC)

In Mandatory Access Control, the definition and implementation of access control policies for the whole system is by the administrators. Once defined, these policies that cannot be evaded by the subjects.MAC policies outdo the DAC file and directory permissions. The mandatory rules of "read up "and "no write down" [84] guarantees security in MAC. SELinux and AppArmor are most widely used MAC technologies for Linux and are applied using Linux Security Modules (LSM) framework.

SELinux

SELinux applies policy-based security controls to define permitted operations for a process on a system regardless of DAC privileges. Labels specify the access policies for complete system elements comprising files, directories, process and container objects. It offers a tough level of container isolation.

AppArmor

AppArmor is a Linux security module (LSM) system. it is a Mandatory Access Control (MAC) model for Linux, with a fine-grained access control that allows an application to access the objects identified in AppArmor Profile. It has a file path based approach, unlike SELinux which has label based method. The enforcement mode of AppArmor imposes policies on an application and alerts any breach. The enforcement mode of AppArmor limits a container from accessing a vital file system on the host in case a compromised container.

Information Flow Control (IFC)

Information Flow Control is a MAC based technique that controls and safeguards the data propagation. IFC assures a restrained and safe information flow using labels attached to the data as well as to the subjects who desire to access the data. The secrecy and integrity labels can be associated with the system entities. Data flow is permitted only if the "security label of the source is a subset of the label of the receiver" [10].

1.3 Cloud Computing for Collaborative Research

Cloud computing propounds the possibilities to review the exploitation of technology in research. Several prospects wait for further open and widespread collaboration by means of virtual research environments and cloud computing services. Mid 1990's saw the rise of grid based e-infrastructures that are comprised of research networks and middleware services to support collaborative sharing of dispersed resources among researchers. Such science gateways catered to the resource requisites for specific and generic research initiatives. With emergence of cloud computing, robust and highly versatile virtual research environments as well as Science Clouds came into existence to further collaborative research [73].

1.3.1 Scope & Opportunity

Cloud-based collaborative research platforms renders computational as well as storage resources essential for running the research tools and applications. Individual research organisations can utilize the huge set of computing resources the cloud platforms offer, scale up and down according to the fluctuating workloads and pay as per the usage. The multitenant cloud architectures could aid multidisciplinary scientific collaboration and empowered data and tool sharing, collaborative application development, experimental data and view or search of datasets [73]. In preference to discrete data management and sharing frameworks, collaborating research institutions currently relies on the cloud services to provision the resource according to the data, compute and resource demanding tools that are shared [34]. Cloud computing offers the researchers an extensive range of instance types that match up with the features of the research tools and applications, thus facilitate the creation of custom built runtime environments.

1.3.2 Research Significance

Scientific research involves data, resource and computationally intensive analyses and experimentations that has erratic requirements for resource [60] [80]. Such research tools and applications causes bursty workloads in the framework [46]. Most of the existing research frameworks follow static resource provisioning, which are inadequate to meet the dynamic resource requirements of the research applications. Hence it is significant to examine the dynamic resource allocation to achieve improved throughput and optimal resource utilization.

1.4 Problem Description

Sharing of confidential research resources using a public network such as internet has always been a concern in collaborative research environments. Although approaches like k-anonymization and differential privacy were used to maintain confidentiality of data, those are not advantageous in collaborative research platforms with multiple researchers sharing the data and applications or tools, along with all its dependencies to foster reproducibility of research. The identified challenges with reference to the above scenario are listed below:

Breach of security and lack of control: The breach of security and lack of control over the shared resources makes the researchers hesitant in sharing data, tools, and inferences with others [13] [55]. It is imperative to apply techniques to guarantee that data and tools are not accessed by unauthorised users and are secured from malicious attacks. Though various solutions have been proposed in literatures, for example [64] [17], to address secure data sharing in collaborative research environments and data owners access control problem, much work does not exist on secured sharing and access control of application or tools.

Resource locking: Static provisioning leads to resource locking that hinders the provisioning to meet up to the varying workloads imposed by resource hungry and computationally intensive analysis tools used in research. Dynamic provision of the computational capacity as per the unpredictable work load that arises in the executions of scientific tools and applications necessitates the avoidance of resource-locking caused by provisioning the resources statically. Additionally, the static provisioning effects underutilization or overutilization is a major concern in the resource allocation process.

Lack of a comprehensive assessment: Static resource provisioning approaches, currently offered by the cloud providers does not comprehensively assess the applications and resources available, but schedule the applications independently which leads to increased execution time for applications [71].

Lack of a flexible, Policy based access control: The original researcher to whom the research resources belong to, should be able to define the policy concerning to the authorisation of users to access the data and applications and the permitted activities on the resources. The coarse grained access control models fail to deliver the passable flexibility that empowers the user to specify the access policies.

This research work, therefore, strives to inquire the solution towards the above-said problems and has designed a framework to expedite collaborative research that rapidly spawns and provisions computational resources to cater the inconsistent workloads and facilitate secured, restrained sharing of data and tools among researchers.

1.5 Research Aim and Objectives

Taking into account the enormous possibilities of Cloud Computing technologies for collaborative research, this research work proposes to undertake the following:

1. Design of a framework based on cloud computing technology, to foster collaborative research that assists researchers to securely share research data, inferences, tools and associated system environment and hence recreate a comprehensive computational environment to run the applications.
2. Design an authentication, authorization framework that offers flexibility and with novel access control mechanism for secure sharing of sensitive research resources and prevent unauthorized access and malicious attacks.
3. To achieve dynamic resource allocation and optimize the resource utilization in the collaborative research framework with respect to throughput and finish time.
4. Evaluate the performance efficiency of the framework and security through a system prototype.

1.6 Motivation

With rapid advancements in technology, contemporary collaborative scientific research has accomplished new dimensions. Science clouds, grid or cluster based research networks, middleware services, scientific workflows, file hosting and content management services etc. have furthered research collaborations. Enormous possibilities offered by cloud computing for collaborative research is well acclaimed. Despite the wide-range of rewards, collaborative platforms face significant challenges, specially concerning to heterogeneity, reproducibility,

resource allocation, access control and security. An in-depth literature review about existing collaborative research frameworks and latest cloud technologies, helped realizing the fact that, there is a significant requirement for prospective research towards the design of a collaborative research framework, exploiting full potential of cloud computing and resolving the recognized problems. The motivation for this research work was derived from the research literatures papers conversed below:
In the research paper [25] Katz et al have brought about an elaborative review and discussion on research collaboration, its paybacks and pitfalls, elements of inspiration and also effects of collaboration on research proficiency. The relevance of data sharing to the scientific research communities have been discussed by Almeida et al [52] and Poldrack et al [53]. Klien [36] have discussed the significance of interdisciplinary collaboration in scientific research. The impulse for a research work as to the design of a collaborative research framework that utilizes the cloud capabilities, was drawn from the research works presented by Yongzheng Ma et al [80], McGregor et al [43] and Wagenaar et al [29].

1.7 Methodology

This research has adopted design science research methodology [70] to accomplish the research objectives. The qualitative analysis comprised of in-depth literature review about existing related works and technologies, together with interview studies, aided in identification of research problems and defining the research objectives. The schematic diagram of adopted research methodology is demonstrated in Figure 1.2. The research work aimed to design and develop a collaborative research cloud framework that mitigates the problems identified. The system prototype was evaluated and comparative analysis and benchmarking performed with the results of the evaluation.

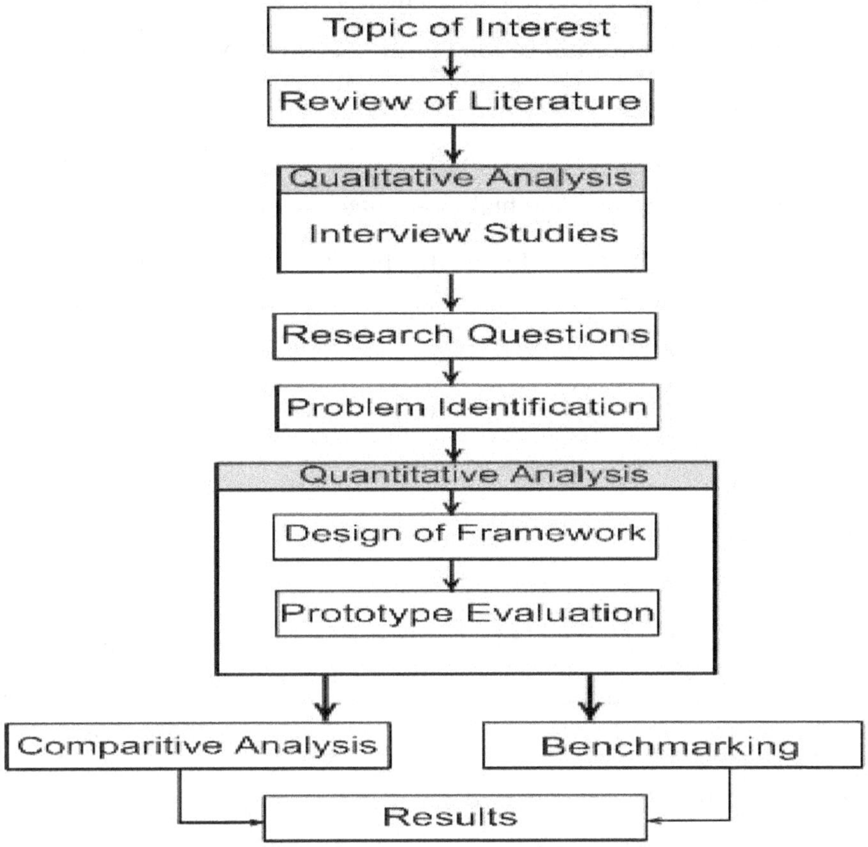

Figure 1. 2 Schematic Diagram of Proposed Research Methodology

According to the above said research methodology the research work can be summarized as below:

- To carry out an investigation on the challenges in collaborative research environments and analyse the techniques used to mitigate the identified problems.
- The authentication, authorization framework of the proposed model enables the research owners and administrators to define and edit the user policies through an interface.
- The dynamic resource provisioning problem is treated as optimization problem which intends to reduce the finish time and increase the throughput to accomplish optimal utilization of resources.
- Develop algorithms for dynamic resource allocation and optimize the resource utilization on collaborative research framework with respect to throughput and finish time. Develop an algorithm that counts on auto-scaling and employs underutilized residual resources to optimize the

resource utilization. A Management Interface (MI) aids the research owner for resource allocation through secured containerization.

- Develop an algorithm for secured object flow control and apply techniques to secure and protect the shared research resources from unauthorized access and malicious attacks.
- Implement a system prototype in OpenStack with Ubuntu and to evaluate performance efficiency and security of the framework through the system prototype. Benchmark the framework with httperf, performing stress tests such as CPU intensive test, Network test and Fork bomb test.

1.8 Thesis Organisation

Chapter-1: Introduction: This chapter will present an introduction to the collaborative research, cloud computing, relevance of cloud computing technology in facilitating academic /scientific collaborative research, the problems being identified, motivation, research goals, etc.

Chapter-2: Literature Review: The chapter will present an extensive literature review to understand the existing previous works and will feature the substantial research gap.

Chapter-3: Collaborative Research Cloud Framework: The chapter will explain the design requirements and high level architecture of the proposed framework. The chapter will also discuss the adopted research methodology and algorithms designed.

Chapter-4: Authentication and Authorisation in Collaborative Research Cloud: The novel user authentication and access control mechanism employed in proposed framework is described in this chapter. Additionally, chapter also presents proposed algorithm for user login process, novel trust model, and hybrid access control approach. The chapter also details the performance analysis, exclusive result analysis and comparative analysis with existing approaches.

Chapter-5: An approach for Optimizing the Dynamic Resource Provisioning in Collaborative Research Cloud: This chapter will discuss dynamic resource provisioning problem in collaborative research cloud and the proposed system model to optimize resource utilization The chapter will also explain the research methodology adopted and algorithms designed, exclusive analysis of data derived from the experiments conducted.

Chapter-6: Security and Isolation in Collaborative Research Cloud: This chapter will discuss the security requirements, vulnerabilities in collaborative research cloud and will elaborate the proposed approach to increase the security and isolation of the shared resources. The chapter will also explain the methodology used and proposed algorithm for secured object flow. The chapter will explain exclusive analysis of data derived from the experiments conducted and benchmarking

Chapter-7: Conclusion. This chapter concludes the thesis, elaborates the contributions of the research and discusses the scope, limitations and future work.

CHAPTER 2

CHAPTER 2

LITERATURE REVIEW

2.1 Preface

This chapter discourses an extensive review of contemporary along with retroactive research works that were surveyed in order to map the advances in the domain of research. The chapter is structured into following sub sections. Section 2.1 summarizes the extant collaborative research frameworks. Section 2.2 deals with review of Virtualization methods and performance evaluation and analysis of the virtualization techniques. Section 2.3 details the review of resource provisioning in virtualized environments. Section 2.4 discusses about the security concerns in cloud environments and prevailing security mechanisms. Section 2.5 highlights the research gaps and Section 2.6 deals with the research questions.

2.2 Collaborative Research Platforms

This section discusses about the existing works related to collaborative research platforms.

In [41] Mardhani et al. have presented a framework for scientific collaboration, motivated by GForge system which is used for collaborative software development. The cluster based framework have abilities to process, store, preserve, and process scientific data.

Sherif et al. [57] proposed a generic collaborative research platform for researchers to utilize remotely located sources of data, dispersed computing locations, range of tools to process and visualize data in neuroimaging research, which is usually resource and compute intensive. This platform integrates the vital features of a grid middleware and have claimed to provide an organized and protected environment.

Marty Humphrey et al. [42] illustrated an approach to overcome the perils in data sharing frameworks .The authors have discussed that most of the grid based frameworks for data sharing, rely much on complex specialized software with interfaces that are not user friendly. They have proposed the design of a generic, cloud based network for exchange of clinical data with a minimum dependency on purpose-built software.

Bastian Roth et al. [8] introduced a collaboration platform for research collaboration with a generic nature, and addresses the many existing challenges in virtual research frameworks that are mostly domain specific. The generic framework leverages on virtues of virtualization technology and groupware tools to resolve the glitches that arise due to software incompatibility, unfamiliar user interfaces, increased cost and difficulty in configuring the hardware infrastructure.

Voss et al. [73] proposed a virtual environment for collaborative research, fully exploiting the elasticity offered by cloud computing to enable automatic provisioning of compute resources. They have discussed that due to the access control method and rapid elasticity of the infrastructure makes it outperform grid or cluster based research environments.

Benjamin H. Brinkman et al. [29] have put forward a cloud-based collaborative research portal for sharing of large EEG datasets along geographically dispersed locations. Authors have discussed that portal delivers the requisites of a collaborative research platform, have drawn attention to the key functionalities for example security of data, access rights, validating and verifying the results of data analysis etc.

McGregor et al. [43] have proposed a platform for researchers to share software tools, bring together dispersed set of heterogeneous resources, thus facilitate effective collaboration and the django-tastypie based authorization framework for controlling the access to data and resources in the platform.

Kalyanam et al. [33] discoursed about a scientific research cloud grounded on an adaptable framework to facilitate management, processing, analyse and visualizing of geospatial data. The platform leverages on cloud computing services for easy disposition of resources and trustworthy replication.

Yongzheng Ma et al. [80] elucidated a platform that unifies resources for data, hardware and software to provide an internet based user-friendly environment, to facilitate technologists spread across the globe to collaborate and work on multidisciplinary applications. The authors have proposed effective, unique methods for online collaborations which can overcome various challenges associated with conventional inline collaborations methods like email.

Muhamad Fitra Kacamarga et al. [46] presented a comprehensive computing platform for bioinformatics research, that exerts lightweight virtualization of Docker containers. The authors have investigated the challenges in VM based approach and pronounces about the efficiency of Docker containers in offering custom -built of the compute environment.

Yujian Zhu et al. [81] have put forward a scalable system established on lightweight Linux Containers, to monitor and bill the usage in datacentres developed to meet resource needs for institutions relating to academic and scientific research.

Musa et al. [24] have introduces a portable platform that wraps the whole set of resources and underlying logic for resource management and endows it to the users. The authors have claimed that the proposed approach based on cloud container technology, mitigates the problems in massive scale data analysis and conducts an efficient resource provisioning with reduced overhead.

Svetlana et al. [62] have remarked that lack of tools to replicate the operating system with all the dependencies is a significant problem in research reproducibility. They have proposed an approach to create a tool based on lightweight virtualisation for reproducing research environments. Linux namespaces are utilized for building the solution and the authors have claimed that such a solution will not interrupt the host operating system.

2.3 Virtualization Techniques

In this section, we reviewed the research papers that have discussed virtualization methods, performance evaluation and analysis of the virtualisation techniques. Our study on the existing approaches and performance evaluation and analysis of the different virtualization methods shows that both hypervisor based and container based virtualization had increased the efficiency than non-virtualized environments.

Nagesh et al. [49] presented a survey of server virtualization, categories of prevalent virtualization techniques, gains, security susceptibility of each method in detail. According to the authors virtualization is an approach of creating many virtual execution environments from a physical server.

Felter et al. [74] attempted a comparative study of performance of Virtual Machines and Linux Containers. KVM virtual machines and Docker containers were exposed to stress tests with set of workloads. According to the authors the, results of the evaluation proved that performance of containers equals the Virtual machines.

According to Miguel G. Xavier et al. [44] though container based system accomplish near-native performance, it is deficient of isolation and security. Authors have discussed about experiments conducted to evaluate the performance efficiency and isolation provided by container-based virtualization and did a comparative study against Xen, a typical hypervisor based virtual system for High Performance Computing. In addition to this, authors have estimated the overhead in HPC with containerised systems, by means of NAS parallel benchmarks. The Figure 2.1 illustrates the performance overhead estimated using NPB benchmarks.

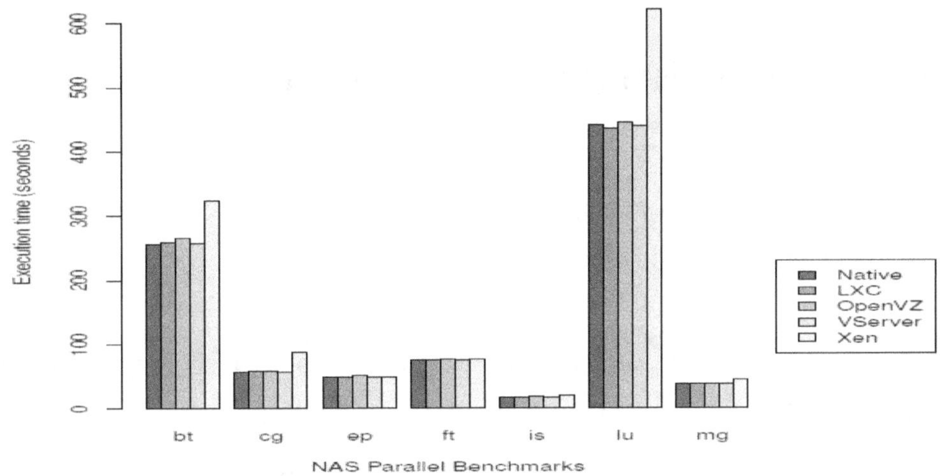

Figure 2. 1 :Comparison of Performance Overhead of Virtualized system with HPC workloads

Sudha et al. [61] performed a comparative study on the performance of KVM and LXC by means of computation and performance test using Apache Benchmark. The authors have discussed that LXC containers surpass KVM and presented a performance closely similar to the host operating system. The review of the paper outlines that Linux Containers are better alternative than hypervisor based KVM due to light weight and better performance.

Zheng Li et al. [82] studied the overhead of LXC containers, in specific Docker containers and compared with that of Virtual machine. Authors explained that lightweight Docker containers is due to the encapsulation of application and all its dependencies. However, they discussed that hypervisor based virtualization may not have a high overhead in all situations.

Jyothi Shetty et al. [30] assessed the virtualization overhead using benchmark (CPU, Disk, Memory) with Phoenix test suite for Docker containers in contrast to VM. According to the authors Docker exceeds VM. On the other hand, containers lack isolation and security level owing to shared host kernel.

2.4 Resource Allocation in Virtualized Environments.

This section presents a comprehensive review of research work about s resource allocation methods used in cloud environments.

Xavier et al. [75] have put forward an algorithm for provisioning resources for collaborative media applications which demands elasticity as well as quality. Authors have argued that the proposed approach is efficient and cost effective than the existing the algorithms, on basis of the results obtained in simulation with CloudSim.

Elaheh kheiri et al. [19] have explained a multitenant resource allocation method and proposed algorithms to mitigate the problems of underutilization and overutilization in resource allocation. According to the authors the proposed approach is cost efficient as well as with meet quality standards. The calculation of response time, server waiting time and availability, in a simulation experiment proves the resource efficiency and effective ness of the model.

Sijin He et al. [59] have introduced an Elastic Application Container to bring in improved resource efficiency and scalability in multi -tenant cloud scenarios. The elaborated that the proposed container based approach has enhanced resource-efficiency in comparison to VM-based approach.

Kimura, et al.[9] have suggested a resource provisioning model for small cloud providers who cannot afford the setup of enormous infrastructures . As stated by the authors, under provisioning and overprovisioning which arises due to resource locking, causes inefficient resource utilization that eventually leads to loss in returns. The proposed system assess the web application workload based on regression method and provisions the virtual machines accordingly.

Ngenzi et al. [3] introduced a framework to improve resource allocation proficiency of virtual machines based on joint operations and decision making. Authors have carried out experiments using math lab to calculate time taken for allocation of a task, wastage of compute power and memory and communication cost. The comparative analysis of above said parameters presented in the paper depicts that proposed framework had a better performance in comparison to existing systems for allocation of resources in cloud based environments.

Guan et al. [77] have presented a discussion about a resource allocation framework deploying Docker containers, to facilitate spontaneous scaling as per the application workload and lessen the cost for provisioning the application in the data centres without forgoing the quality requisites. The paper also proposes an algorithm for resource provisioning in datacentre that host varied application with dynamic resource requirements and enormous physical resources. Authors have discussed that the resource allocation problem is modelled an optimization problem and the approach outperformed virtual machine based approaches, in view of the parameters, cost and acceptance ratio.

Ye Tao [79] et al. have discussed the resource allocation problem in container based frameworks and proposed a node selection algorithm based on fuzzy logic for deploying the containers. The paper discusses the scheme of the framework and the procedures adopted and the work flow in detail. However, the apart from response time, paper does not illustrate any other parameters evaluated.

Garcia et al. [37] have presented an elaborate discussion on the challenges in scheduling and provisioning resources for science clouds. Authors have discussed problems related to resource allocation to meet the demands of scientific application with adhoc requirements, from cloud service provider's perspective. The paper also described the significance of co-allocation mechanism and challenges regarding co-allocation in a cloud system. According to the authors, it is very important for science clouds to follow a resource allocation strategy that is conscious about the performance of the system. Additionally, they discussed existing works and challenges concerning policies for flexible resource allocation, predictability of performance.

2.5 Security

A comprehensive review of research works conducted on security vulnerabilities in cloud environments and existing security mechanisms are presented in this section.

Amara et al. [47] have elaborated the security requirements, threats, security violations in cloud computing systems. They have also presented a detail review of the several techniques to mitigate the attacks. Authors have summarized the categories of security attacks in terms of the different levels, like network, application etc.

Gholami et al. [21] have carried out a detail review of traditional and contemporary technologies on cloud security and privacy. Authors have presented discussion on prevailing methods to safeguard sensitive data in cloud domains.

Disha et al. [45] have presented a study on security problems in different cloud models. They have discussed the issues and effects of various cloud deployment models. Additionally, the susceptibility of virtualization with regard to cloud service models has been elaborated. However, the paper lacks clarity regarding the conclusions derived from the study.

Chelladhurai et al. [27] have conversed the security concerns of Docker containers and presented an elaborate review of the existing works on the same. Authors have listed down security approaches prevalent today to mitigate the security vulnerabilities of Docker. Authors have presented a theoretical discussion on proposed method to encounter Dos (Denial of Service). Authors have conducted experimental study through execution of proposed model for various test cases.

Thangapandiyan et al. [40] have proposed a framework that provide privacy, trust and security from adversaries. The focus of paper is in delivering a trust management model as service for the providers as well as users. Authors noted that, suitability of the proposed framework was investigated with real time user responses.

Takabi et al. [22] have presented a theoretical discussion on fundamental cloud concepts, issues on security and privacy in cloud implementations, Access control mechanisms and trust management. Additionally, authors have also given a brief discussion regarding heterogeneity about semantics of policies.

Thilakanathan et al [64] have demonstrated an elaborate review on security of shared data by the use of cloud. The paper has discussed the concerns in sharing of information and significance of retaining privacy and secrecy of shared data in various domains like healthcare, government etc. Authors have noted the kinds of attacks, cloud systems are vulnerable to and what stimulate the adversaries for these attacks. They have presented a number of real word examples of the issues. The significance of data sharing for the organisations and prerequisites to facilitate the data exchange, has been elaborated in the paper. Authors have presented an in-depth review of existing encryption based methodologies to enable information sharing.

Nepal [54] et al. have proposed trusted storage cloud for scientific workflows, which tackles integrity, confidentiality and availability of the data and additionally an access control mechanism to secure and authorize the sharing of sensitive data to enable collaboration among multiple researchers. According to the authors, store level access control maintains an Access Control List (ACL)with usernames and their access levels. The paper also depicts how the proposed the architecture fosters collaborative research in bioinformatics.

Gonzales et al.[18] have presented a framework that evaluate the security offered by the cloud service provider in terms of confidentiality and integrity. The proposed assessment model calculates the level of security, that can be used by cloud tenants to select an Infrastructure as service cloud service provider based on the security preferences. Authors have explained that the trust model determines the chances of advanced persistent threats in cloud computing systems.

Danan Thilakanathan et al. [17] have introduced a solution for safe sharing of information in collaborative environments grounded on cloud. According to the authors, in the proposed approach data to be shared is encrypted and policies specified on who and how the data will be accessed are safely packaged into an object. They have noted that data owner specifies using XACML policy language, Policy definition points (PDP)in the object infers the policies and policy enforcement point (PEP) imposes the policy.

Chen et al. [78] have proposed an architecture built on software and hardware that bundles data and policies for access control and delivers it to legitimate users and applications to render an improved access control. The solution attaches the policies as hardware tags to the data. The authors have claimed that this approach effectively averts un authorised secondary propagation of shared data.

Pasquier et al. [65] introduced a model to establish the possibility of implementing Information flow control (IFC) being a part of cloud framework to provide a secure and elastic data sharing beyond the isolation boundaries. The authors have noted that the proposed platform assist in managing the data and securing the application from malicious code. A detail study of existing isolation techniques is also presented. The paper has also explained how Information flow can be applied in Linux kernel as security module.

Gonzales et al. [12] introduced a benchmark to evaluate and relate various virtualized systems to enable cloud providers to decide on the right system. The assessment process examines occurrence of weaknesses and reliability of the cloud system.

Denning [15] have studied techniques which assures secured flow of information. Author have evaluated the security requites using a lattice based mathematical model. The proposed model is relevant to be applied for limiting a process from leakage of sensitive information regarding a client application.

Myers et al. [10] proposed a decentralized Information Flow Control (IFC) model that defines secrecy and integrity labels linked to system objects and data flow is permitted only "if the security label of the source is a subset of the label of the receiver". According to the authors, the approach guarantees a cost-effective and time efficient solution for regulated information flow devoid of stringent controls in a system.

Bacon et al. [26] have inspected the practicability of positioning IFC embodied in the cloud framework itself. Authors have noted the suitability and potential of decentralized IFC models for academic research ventures. The paper has explained various aspects of cloud security with respect to data and reviewed existing as well as proposed work on Information flows control. They have also emphasized on the need of setting up policies on security between the providers and the users. Authors also noted the concerns related to IFC implementation.

Pasquier et al. [66] have discussed the isolation provided by container technology and hypervisor based virtual machines. The proposed IFC empowered cloud model offers secured and elastic data sharing. The paper has carried out a comparison of isolation of containers and proposed IFC-enabled operating system model.

Sandhu et al. [56] have explained what is access control and how is it relates to other security mechanisms. Authors have presented a theoretical analysis of existing policies for access control and administration.

Ferraiolo et al. [57] have emphasized on the definition, applicability and unique features of Role-Based Access Control (RBAC). Authors have stated that RBAC is nondiscretionary access control method that allows access to the resources based on the subject's role in an organization. The paper discussed the dissimilarities between RBCA and Discretely Acess Control (DAC). The Study also depicts the competencies of RBAC in managing organisational security.

Dalton et al. [58] introduced a method for resolving risks related to user authentication and authorisation in web-apps. The proposed approach dynamically tracks the flow of information to ensure only authenticated users gain access to the confidential data and resources. The paper also noted that the prototype evaluation proved the efficiency of the proposed model for deploying secured authentication and access control for web applications.

Alobaidan et al. [23] emphasized on the trust based model to mitigate risks related to weak isolation provided by containers with Operating system level virtualization. Authors have proposed a trust model that enhance the isolation of containers and hence the security using Role-based Access Control (RBAC). The paper also illustrated benchmarking experiments conducted to investigate the isolation of containers in comparison with conventional Virtual machines.

Balamurugan et al. [70] have introduced an access control scheme that combines DAC concepts to RBAC. Access Control List and Access Control Matrix are used along with RBAC for improving the integrity of data. The paper noted only theoretical details of evaluation and lacks the results of comparative study and experiments.

Win et al. [67] proposed an approach to defend guest containers from attacks where malicious host get the access to the containers and alters it, specifically in container virtualized systems. Authors have studied the weaknesses of namespace isolation in Linux kernels. They have proposed an approach with Mandatory Access Control based Apparmor along with system call interception to resolve the above issue. According to the authors the solution efficiently controls "Host break in" with a minimal overhead.

Anh et al. [69] have presented a framework to facilitate safe sharing of data in cloud. Authors have explained that the proposed framework is user friendly and elastic that let the data owners to specify the access policies. The framework leverages on XACML for policy specification to enable a fine grained access control. The prototype of the framework was evaluated based on time to complete a request and compared with a native system.

Gao et al. [76] have investigated the sources of information loss in a container based cloud systems. According to the authors such pathways are easily accessible for malicious intruders to create attacks that affects the system reliability. They have proposed a security scheme to secure from advanced attacks and increase the confidentiality and integrity of the system with a minimum overhead.

Sarkale et al. [72] have introduced a framework to increase the security of cloud containers by enforcing access control and monitoring module. According to the authors, containers lack an added layer of isolation delivered by the hypervisor which makes it easy for adversaries to launch into the host machine. Cloud container based environments that lack strong access control policies are vulnerable to attacks that causes advisories to attach client-end script to the web pages. In the framework container profiles are verified against defined policies to ensure security and anomalous containers are black listed and will be denied access. The authors have discussed that their proposed security layer assure protection from security attacks like kernel exploits and container breakout that may occur in systems based on container based virtualization.

2.6 Qualitative Analysis

Interview was conducted with thirty users from twenty organizations in healthcare, retail and educational domains, who has moved their application to private / public cloud. The organizations moved some of the on-premise applications to cloud. These thirty users were decision makers for the process of moving the applications to cloud.

The questions asked to the respondents were:

1) Why did you move to cloud and which attributes of cloud are important for you?
    a. Adhoc scalability
    b. Cost
    c. Security
    d. QOS
    e. easier collaboration
2) What do you think is the severity of the following security threats in your cloud environment?
    a. Identity and Access Management (IAM)
    b. Data Leakage/Protection
    c. Denial Of Service attack
    d. Network security
    e. Data retrieval
3) Which among these attributes poses challenges in collaborative research environments?
    a. IAM
    b. Auto scaling
    c. Monitor and control
    d. Control over Data/Tools
    e. Security

Table 2. 1: Factors for Cloud Adoption

Important factors to move to cloud	Education	Retail	Healthcare
Adhoc scalability	10	10	6
Cost	6	6	5
Security	3	2	2
QOS	5	7	8
Easier collaboration	6	5	9

Table 2.1 illustrates how many users in each domain considered a particular factor as important feature of the organisational cloud. The quantitative value indicates the number of respondents.

The analysis of data shows that in educational sector, the major reason for cloud adoption is due to the factors adhoc scalability, cost and easier collaboration. In retail sector, the respondents considered scalability and QOS as important but for users from healthcare QOS and easiness for collaboration were the essential factors. Figure 2.2 illustrates the comparative analysis of data collected from interview studies for the first question.

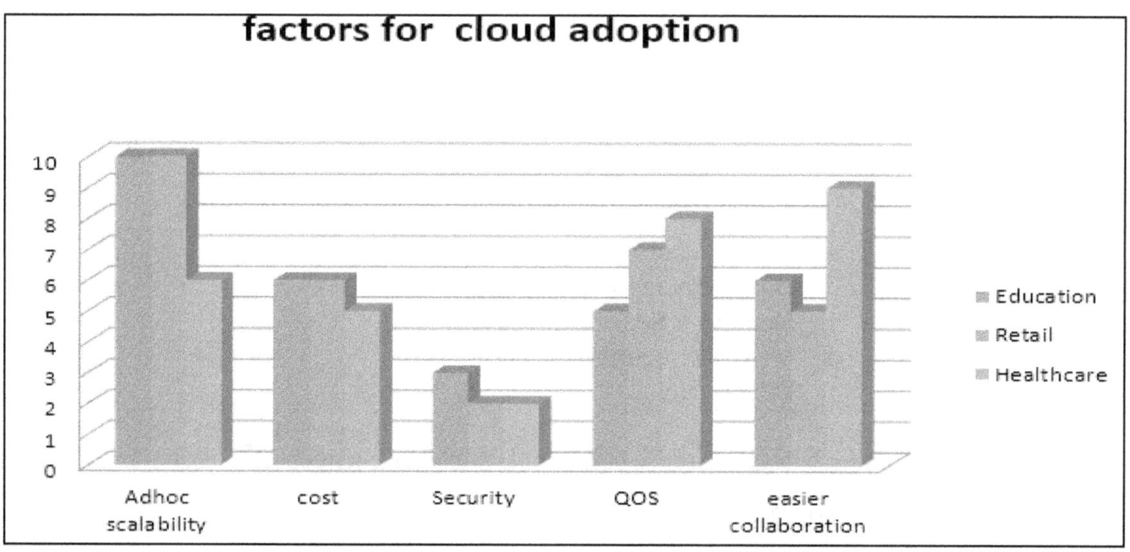

Figure 2. 2 Data Analysis of Interview Studies for Cloud Adoption Factors

Table 2.2 shows the users response to question Q2 regarding the security threats in cloud systems.

Table 2. 2: Threats in Cloud Adoption

Threats impacting Cloud	Education	Retail	Healthcare
IAM	17	22	20
Data Leak	25	30	30
Denial Of service	15	18	17
Network Security	20	25	28
Data retrieval	20	25	28

Analysis of data of cloud Table 2.3 shows that users in all the three sectors thought data leakage as an important issue in cloud systems. They also looked at network security and data retrieval as major concerns in public clouds. Figure 2.3 demonstrates the data analysis of interview studies on threats in cloud systems.

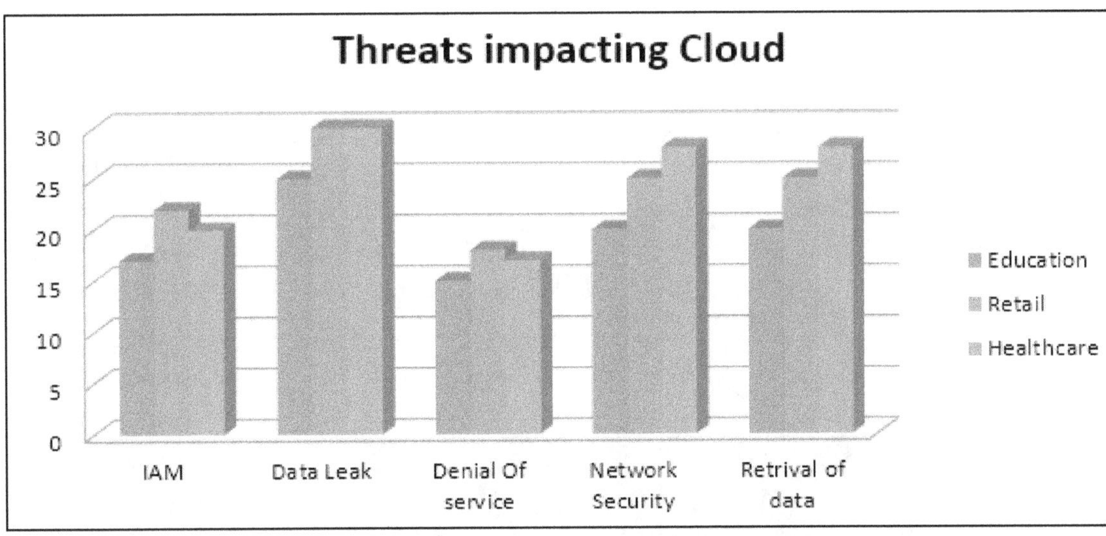

Figure 2. 3 : Data Analysis of Interview studies on Threats in Cloud systems

Table 2.3 shows the respondents response to question Q3 which deals with challenges in cloud based collaborative research.

Table 2. 3: Challenges in Collaborative Research Environments

Collaborative research challenges	Education
IAM	12
Auto scaling	13
Monitor and control	15
Control over Data/Tools	20
Security	20

According to twenty respondents from different organisation in education and research, control over sensitive shared data and proprietary tools and security are major concerns to addressed. Data analysis of Table 2.3 is illustrated in Figure 2.4.

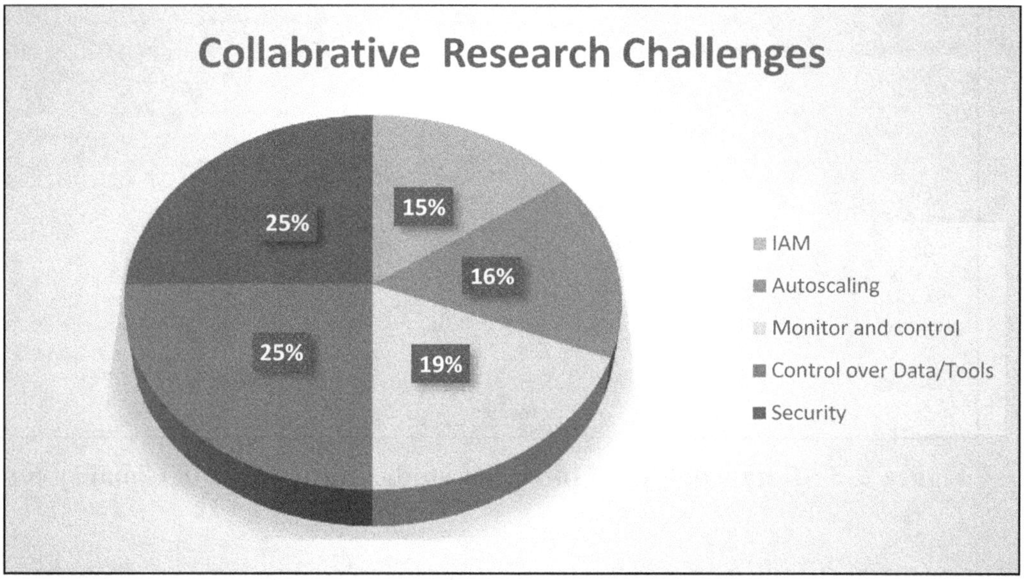

Figure 2. 4: Data Analysis of Interview studies

2.7 Research Gaps

It is obvious from the literature review that there have been many research works aiming to deliver a comprehensive environment for collaborative research.

However, there exist some significant problems that need to be addressed. The existing research gaps are summarized as follows:

Lack of a flexible access control policy approach: Many existing research works on collaborative research cloud has discussed about access control policies employed in their framework. But most of them are role specific and does not offer the flexibility that allows the owners to define the policy regarding authorisation and permitted actions on the resources.

Less attention given or monitoring and control of shared resources: The original researchers to whom the data, tools, and results belong to, are uncertain about the control over the resources that are distributed among multiple users in collaborative research environments. Even though many techniques are available to monitor and control shared data or tools in collaborative environments, very less research papers have discussed about deployment of such capabilities in a collaborative research clouds.

Lack of a mathematical modelling for optimization of resource allocation in collaborative research clouds: Another important observation is that many research papers have discussed resource provisioning in cloud systems and have used algorithms to optimize the performance in terms of various parameters. But none of the papers have discussed a mathematical model for dynamic resource allocation in research clouds with highly variable workloads.

2.8 Research Questions

The research questions considered for the proposed study are listed as below:

RQ1: Can a cloud framework be designed with flexible fine grained access control to foster collaborative research?

RQ2: How to optimize the resource utilization in a compute environment that rapidly allocates resources according to the application needs?

RQ3: How to secure the shared research resources from unauthorised access and malicious attacks?

The major contribution of this thesis would be to study the above said research questions, and address the identified issues.

2.9 Summary

This chapter has presented a near exhaustive review of existing research literatures in collaborative research frameworks, virtualization approaches, resource provisioning in virtualized systems, security problems in cloud environments and security mechanisms. The chapter has also discussed the details of interview studies conducted in different organisations belonging to education, retail and healthcare regarding various concerns in cloud adoption and challenges in cloud based collaborative research. The chapter has also outlined the identified research gaps and research questions framed.

CHAPTER 3

CHAPTER 3

COLLABORATIVE RESEARCH CLOUD FRAMEWORK

3.1 Preface

The chapter will explain the design requirements and high level architecture of the proposed Collaborative Research Cloud (CRC) framework. The chapter will also discuss the adopted methodology and sequence of operations in the entire framework.

3.2 Research Problem

A collaborative research cloud framework should facilitate researchers from various organizations and domains to work together and share data and tools. Researchers may desire to focus on domain of research instead of being adept in infrastructure installations and analysis tools. The framework ought to assist the sharing of data, heterogeneous tools and applications among researchers using dissimilar computing platforms. The framework should spawn different environments, which create results for the different parameters and thus emulate the research environment independent of the platform.

Some of the issues to be addressed while designing the framework is as follows:

- Several frameworks based on cloud computing are extant to aid research collaboration, however many of such frameworks are not adequately flexible to allow the researchers to select resources as per to his research requirements.
- The computational tools or applications deployed for scientific research analysis are firmly coupled with system and registry settings. This necessitates the replicating of the system settings to deploy the analysis tools and applications that are shared among researchers.

- Existing collaborative research platforms are yet to embrace research reproducibility as it demands platform configurations, virtual machine clustering, resolving OS compatibility, additional software libraries and tools.

3.3 Proposed Methodology

The primary objective of the research is to design a cloud based framework to further collaborative research, that enable the researchers to emulate the shared tools and applications to run self-reliantly in a secure environment. Design science research methodology is adopted in this research work which consists of analysis of the design requirements of the framework and development of a conceptual model of the same.

3.3.1 Design Considerations

The following section describes some of the key design requirements that has helped to evolve up with the research cloud framework.

- **Flexibility**: Scientific research analysis necessitates recreation of multiple environments and spawn results for different parameter settings. Researchers may have the need to recreate a system environment of an existing project, through duplication of the system settings regardless of the local host environment [66]. The proposed framework strives to offer a platform to execute application instances multiple times for different users, and thus assists researchers to collaborate on a project.
- **Reproducibility:** The proposed framework requires to endorse reproducibility to enable the recreation of the computational environment as employed by the original owner of the research work. This is achieved by employing lightweight cloud containers that packages requested data, application or tools for analysis and with all dependencies, hence the entire project workflow could be reproduced and extended to the collaborating researchers. This expedites validation of the already available results and inferences and further inventive analysis.

- **Computational portability:** The analysis tools or applications used in scientific research are usually closely coupled to system and registry settings. Sharing of tools to advance inventive analysis also demands reproduction of the system settings to run these applications The proposed framework has employed platform independent, portable, lightweight containers to enable the exporting of the application instances.
- **Dynamic resource provisioning**: Due to the resource and computer heavy tools, applications or data, the resource provisioning faces challenges arising from bursty workloads [67]. The varied workload that arises because of the intensity of analysis calls for dynamic provisioning of the compute capacity. This necessitates to eliminate resource locking caused due to statically provisioning the resources. The framework counts on cloud scalability to allocate resources responding to the ambiguous workload. Furthermore, a resource provisioning strategy according to the demand variation is employed to commissions or decommissions resource according to the varying demands. The research owner packages requested data, results, and tools along with the dependencies and assigns it to the authorized researcher upon request. The resource allocation is accomplished using containerization.
- **Customization**: In the CRC cloud framework, every authentic researcher is allotted customized containers with applications, results, data, and required compute and storage resource on demand, which can run independent of the environment. The proposed CRC framework banks on secured containerization for allocation of sensitive research data and resources.

3.4 High Level Architecture of Collaborative Research Cloud Framework

The architectural overview shown in Figure 3.1 depicts a plausible scheme, where research owner (original researcher to whom research resources belong to) allocates the resources in a secured container named as RCU (Research Collaboration Unit), upon receiving a request from an authorized user. The proposed architecture facilitates researchers to share resources bundled in secured containers, control and monitor the propagation of data and tools and define an access control policy for the objects shared in collaborative research cloud. The flexible user access control module implemented in authentication and authorization framework enables collaborative access and support multi-policy. The flexibility of the access control model empowers research owner to set access policy rights based on the roles and requirements of the different researchers. Contrasting to the extant cloud frameworks that facilitates research collaboration, proposed framework empowers the researchers to select the required resources and researcher owners to define access privileges on his resources.

Many existing approaches has used IFC (Information Flow Control) to control and monitor data flow and control its propagation and the proposed approach has extended this capability to control the propagation of containers that enclose resources. The detail enumeration of the architectural components of CRC framework is given in subsequent sections of this chapter.

3.5 Architectural Overview of CRC Framework

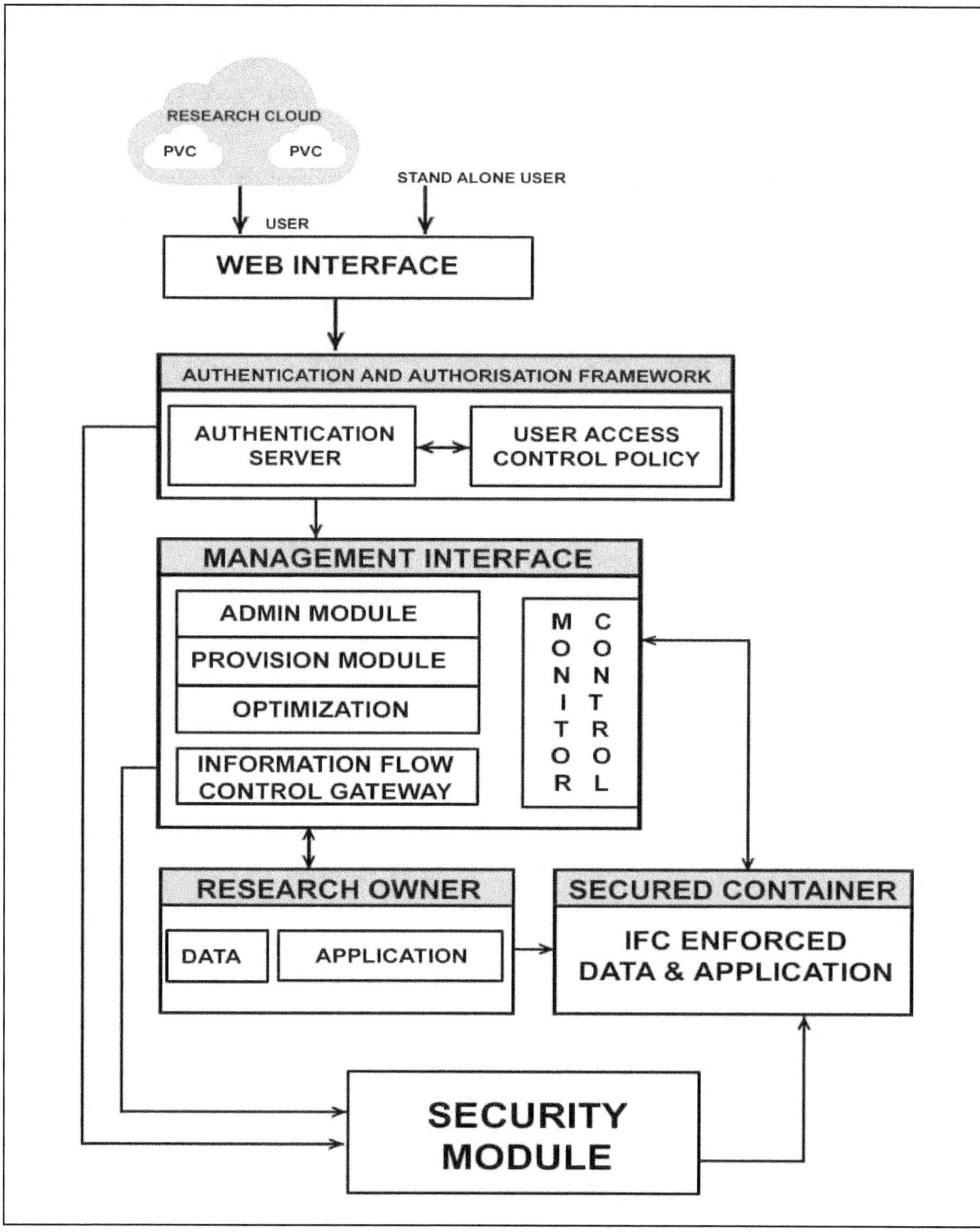

Figure 3. 1 Architectural Overview of CRC Framework

3.5.1 Research Collaboration Unit (RCU)

The conceptual model of custom built container with data, applications/ tools, operating system and all such dependencies is defined as RCU. The RCU is empowered to run application instances and create operating images for the researcher. Figure 3.2 illustrates a conceptual model of an RCU. The proposed model assists rapid spawning of compute instances and deliver a custom-built unit of resources as requested by the researcher.

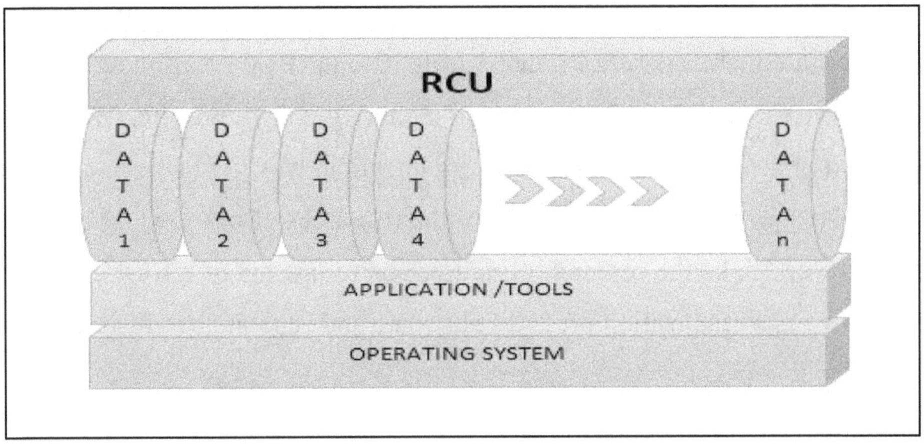

Figure 3. 2: Model of RCU

.

3.5.2 Management Interface (MI)

The researcher to whom the data, analysis tools and application or inferences belongs to, is defined as Research Owner (RO). The management, administering and provisioning of RCU is realized through MI. The admin module reviews and evaluates the resources utilization. The RCU resources considered can be memory, storage space, or compute power. RO defines the access policies on each RCU using the admin module. The provision module sends the researchers request to RO. When RO approves the request, MI verifies the resources availability with RO and provisions the RCU and assigns the RCUs to researcher. RO is entitled to create fixed number of RCU and provision module accomplishes the optimal usage of the resources. Once the resource utilization of the assigned RCU reaches the maximum, unutilized resources of other RCUs are used. MI also utilizes the available residual resources available in CRC and allocates to RCU that demands it so as to achieve a faster execution time. Information Flow Control endows controlled and safe information flow by attaching labels with resources and users who wish to access the resources.

3.5.3 Private Virtual Cloud (PVC)

In the proposed model, the Private cloud of a participating organization is defined as OU (Organizational Unit) that follows a hierarchical structure based on the roles of researcher's role in the research cloud. All participating research organizations are members of a Private Virtual Cloud (PVC) configured on cloud platform services like OpenStack, Open Nebula, AWS Azure etc. PVC is the private cloud of the participating research organization. PVCs are able to cloudburst to many trusted private clouds, to improve the resources utilization. The research cloud framework links the research organisations by means of a trust established network. Network virtualization provides adequate and separate bandwidth for each link.

3.5.4 Authentication and Authorization Framework

Authentication defines the user identity prior to log in process and authorization decides on the user's access privileges to the system resources. The proposed authentication and authorization framework authenticates any researcher who wish to login to participating PVCs and authorises him to access the resources of CRC. The proposed approach integrates Role Based Access Control and Access Control List. Such an integrated approach improves the integrity of data as well as resources. Robust authentication mechanisms and access control rules resolves several security problems that are caused due to multi-tenancy in cloud based systems and non-implementation of trust mechanisms.

3.5.5 The Security Module

The proposed framework applies techniques to guarantee that data and tools are not retrieved by unauthorised users and are protected from illegal activities. The methodology relies on employing robust access control mechanism combined with Process ID (PID) isolation to elucidate the security challenges instigated due to a shared kernel. The augmentation of the isolation and security of the cloud container-based environment facilitate the safe sharing of the sensitive research data and applications across such public hosted collaboration platforms with a strong access control approach that promises confidentiality and authorized access.

3.6 Sequence Diagram of CRC

The flow of actions during a request –response between R_n and RO is as illustrated in Figure 3.4. The stepwise explanation of the sequence diagram is given below:

Step 1: Researcher R_n demand for resources through Manage Interface(MI).

Step 2: MI authenticates researcher R_n.

Step 3: MI directs resource request to RO.

Step 4: RO verifies the request, authenticate and allocate resources wrapped in RCU.

Step 5: Register RCU details (memory, CPU, storage, bandwidth) with MI.

Step 6: Researcher access privileges on RCU is set and granted to the researcher.

Step 7: Researcher access RCU.

Step 8: MI monitors RCU performance for under provisioning or over provisioning.

Step 9: MI manages RCU the resource and resource allocation.

Step 10: MI optimizes RCU for better finish time and resource utilization.

Step11: Researcher sends the decommission request to MI upon finishing the job.

Step 12: MI decommissions RCU by releasing the resources.

Step 13: MI update the resource pool of RCU.

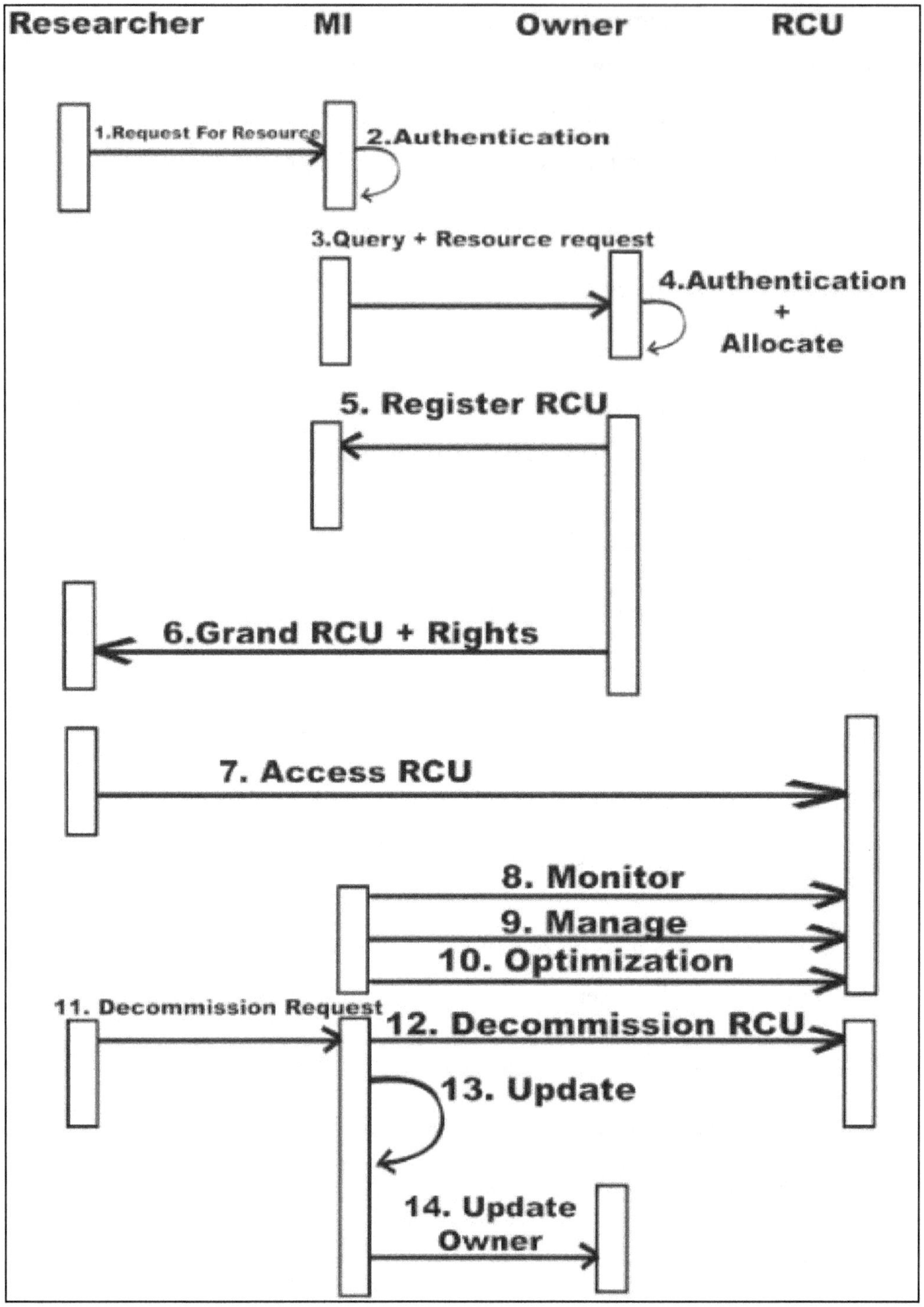

Figure 3. 3 : Sequence diagram of CRC

3.7 Summary

This chapter has presented a discussion on designing the Collaborative Research Cloud (CRC) framework to support collaborative research and enable the researchers to securely share sensitive research data, applications as well as able to emulate the shared tools, independent of the platform, for further ingenious analysis of data. The proposed framework has applied a novel access control model to authenticate and authorize the researchers from heterogeneous organizations to collaborate and access the resources of collaborative research cloud.

CHAPTER 4

CHAPTER-4

AUTHENTICATION AND AUTHORISATION IN COLLABORATIVE RESEARCH CLOUD

4.1 Preface

This chapter will discuss in detail the authentication and authorization process in the proposed collaborative research cloud framework. The chapter also discusses the algorithms designed for user creation and login process. The exclusive analysis of data derived from the experiments conducted, performance analysis of collaborative research cloud framework and comparative analysis with existing systems are presented in the chapter.

4.2 Research Problem

Authenticating the researchers to the research cloud is yet another important issue to be addressed. The proposed authentication and authorization framework should make sure that only authenticated users are able to access the research cloud. An appropriate authentication mechanism need to be adopted for verifying the genuineness of the users from heterogeneous private clouds of the participating organizations. Authorization is a vital mechanism to minimize the security and privacy threats that are caused in multitenant cloud environments. An access control model also ensures only authenticated users are permitted to perform operations according to the defined access privileges.

4.3 Methodology

The proposed framework deploys an authentication and authorization sever that integrates multiple heterogeneous authentication mechanisms used by the participating organizations. The proposed trust model permits a trusted user to single sign on to his PVC and access to any other participating organization's resources. The authentication mechanism counts on the proposed algorithm that authenticates a user in two levels, at the user level and group level. The schematic diagram of the proposed methodology for authentication and authentication is as presented in Figure 4.1.

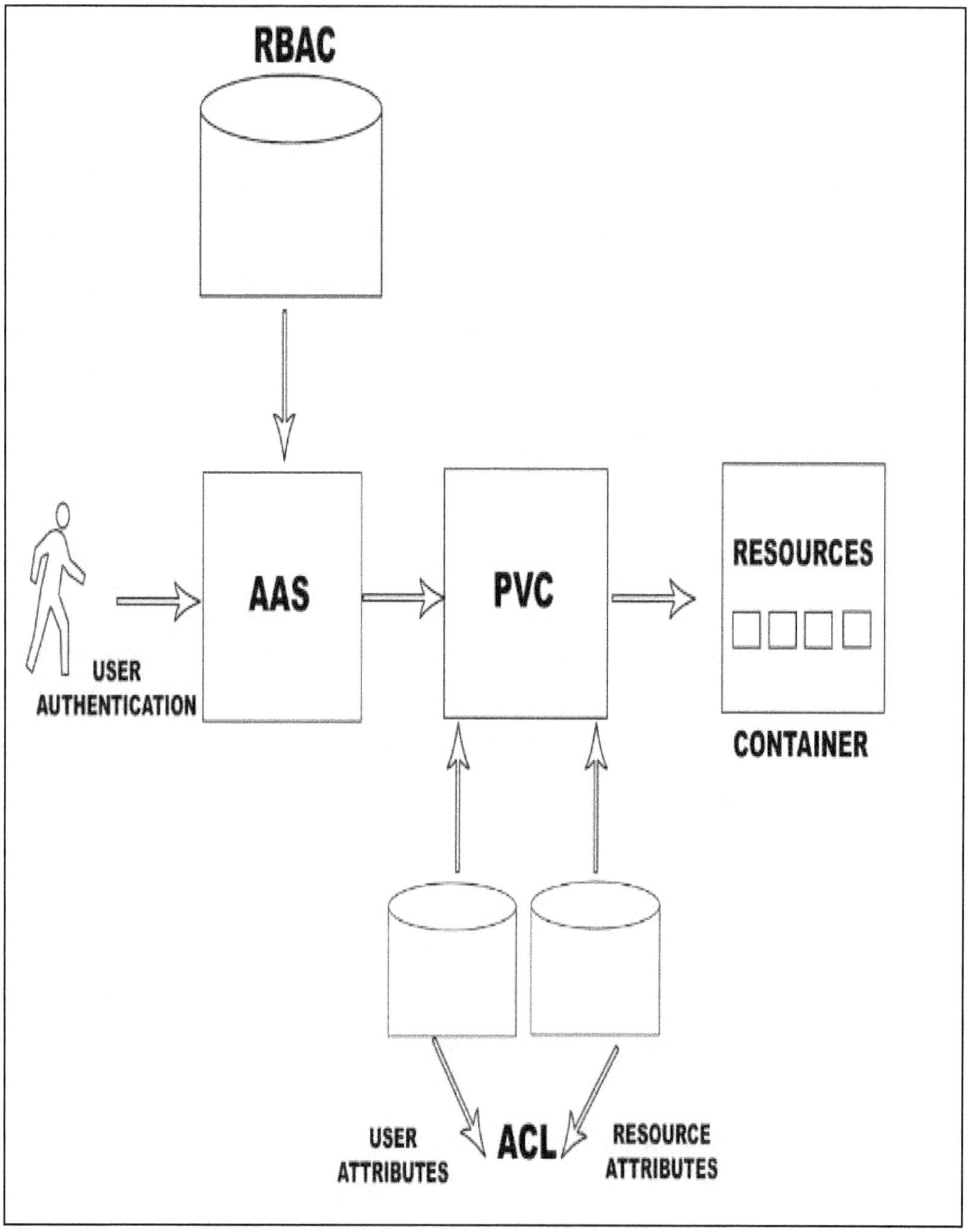

Figure 4. 1: Architectural Overview of Authentication-Authorisation Framework of CRC

4.3.1 LDAP Directory Structure for PVC

The private cloud of a participating organization adapts a hierarchical structure based on the researcher's role in the research cloud. The collaborating research organizations are members of a PVC.

Lightweight directory access protocol (LDAP) is platform independent external authentication protocol based on the X.500 Directory Access protocol for authentication. An individual PVC retains a directory that holds user's data in LDAP, that verifies the researchers in accessing the resources.

Research Cloud domains (RC_1, RC_2...) are created for the participating PVCs as Domain Controllers DC. Collaborative Research and DC.Org. Researcher's group based to the research domain are GID_1, GID_2... GIDn. Every researcher in research cloud has a unique identification number named as UID_1, UID_2... UID_n. Any researcher R_1 can be identified as OU= RC_1, GID=1 and UID=1. A researcher belonging to DC. Collaborative research is represented as R_n. Resource owner (RO), may also be any R_n. RCx is a PVC participating in DC. Collaborative Research. The directory topology of contributing PVC's LDAP server is illustrated in Figure 4.2

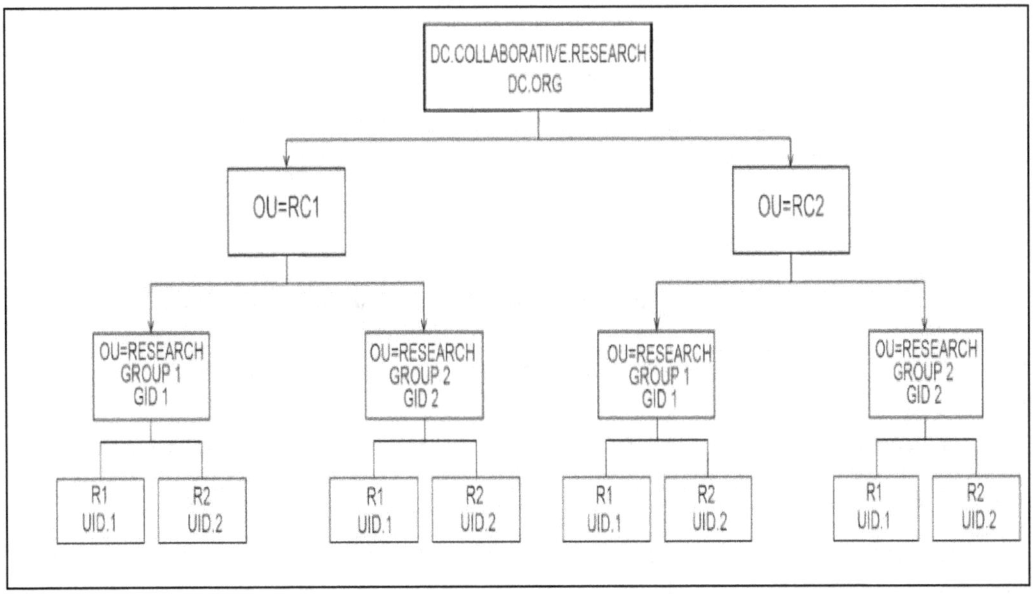

Figure 4. 2: LDAP directory structure for PVC

4.3.2 Authentication and Authorisation Server (AAS)

The authentication and authorisation of a researcher in CRC is done through Authentication and Authorisation Server (AAS) that is constituted as a centralized LDAP server, that maintains the user-id and passwords for CRC. The definition of a collaborating researcher's role in CRC is done in home PVC. AAS authenticates any researcher who wish to login to participating PVCs and approves him to access the resources of CRC. Researcher R_1 with UID=1 and GID=1 access resources in home RC_1 and is allowed to access RCx also. CRC connects diverse research organisations (PVCs) with divergent authentication methods. The peer-to-peer architecture followed in AAS server to network the PVCs, enables easy sync of all other LDAP directories. Hence, AAS functions as an entity for external authentication. The user privileges are defined by integrating /etc /password and ACL (Access control List) directory.

4.4 Trust Model in AAS

Trust establishment between participating PVCs is bidirectional or unidirectional. For example, Trust defined between two organisational units RC_1 and RC_2 is illustrated in Table 4.1. The assumptions for the trust model are : r denote role of a researcher in his home organisation, p denote access permissions of the researcher.

Table 4. 1: Trust established between any two PVC.

	Uni-directional Trust	**Bi-directional Trust**
Trust relationship	RC_1	RC_1 trust RC_2
Trust assignment	RC_1	RC_2 trust RC_1
Authorisation	RC_1	RC_1, RC_2
Permission Assignment	RC_2..r→ RC_2 .p	RC_1.r→ RC_1.p RC_2.r→ RC_2.p

Role hierarchy	$RC_2 \leq RC_1$	$RC_{12}.r \leq RC_1.r$ $RC_1.r \leq RC_2.$
Login	Centralized	Centralized

4.5 Hybrid Access Control Approach in CRC

The collaborative research cloud framework ought to expedite the secured sharing of resources and ensure protection to the shared resources from access unauthorised users. The granular access control method set out in CRC unifies advanced access control approach offered by RBAC (Role Based Access Control) with traditional Discretionary Access Control (DAC) grounded ACL (Access control list) to reinforce the confidentiality and privacy of the resources and sensitive data.

Even though containers forwards the resource allocation and does not add on any additional overheads to the system, the dearth in level of isolation given to shared data and application, need to be resolved in highly sensitive research cloud. The proposed framework mitigates this problem by enhancing the Access control system through the integration of RBAC and ACL. Such an integrated approach improves the integrity of data as well as resources [7] [50].

In the proposed approach a researcher's access rights in AAS is set using RBAC and access rights on the resources is defined using ACL in PVC. Depending on the role of a researcher in his participating organization the access rights are is defined using RBAC. To deal with heterogeneous nature of CRC, all LDAP servers of the collaborating organizations PVCs are synced with AAS. R_n will have privileges in his home RC_n.

The access rights of a researcher R_n to any other RC_X participating in the CRC is set in AAS using RBAC. R_n views abstract of research works available in the RC_x. The access privileges of researcher R_n with GID =x and UID = n and DC. Collaborative research is reflected in the AAS respectively. The novel feature of proposed access control model is that Research Owner (RO) is privileged to define the Access Control Matrix(ACM) for resources in the granted RCU.

The RO can define a researcher's access rights on the granted RCU using ACL, through MI. When a request for resources is received from R_n, RO verifies access privileges and policies defined for R_n and creates the Access Control List

(ACL). Therefore, the entire ownership privileges of the RCU is with the Research Owner.

RO decides on how the access privileges need to be granted to R_n.RO may give the researcher complete access rights on shared RCU objects and revokes rights on RCU or Rn and RO collaborates with equal privileges on RCU.

The access control model is further augmented to incorporate more scalability and flexibility and to meet up dynamic research requirements in a collaborative research environment, which is discussed in detail in Section 6.4. The different types of access rights that are possible using the proposed model are as shown in the Table 4.2.

Table 4. 2: Access Privileges on RCU

Privileges	Description
No Access	Researcher does not view or access to RCU.
View	Researcher can view the RCO content .
View and execute	Researcher has view and execute rights on RCU .
Ownership	RCU is owned by the researcher.

4.6 Algorithm Implementation

This section discourses about the algorithm designed for user creation and login in CRC. The working of the algorithm is based on the trust model discussed above. The authentication mechanism using user id and password has many security concerns, especially in collaborative cloud environments. The proposed algorithms further secure the authentication process and ensures only trusted users are authenticated to research cloud. The explanation of this algorithm is as follows:

4.6.1 Algorithm for User Creation and Login in AAS.

When a researcher's user credentials are created in a research group belonging to a specific domain with UID and GID, concurrently his home directory profile is set in participating PVC. The user should be a researcher under a research group with access rights to the CRC, to access the resources of CRC. In that condition his user profile in home PVC will be synced to AAS user profile. The role and permissions and of the researcher in home RC is permitted to be mapped to any other RC he wants to access.

Algorithm 1: Algorithm for user creation and login in AAS

Assumptions (n: user ID, x: group ID, R_{nx} is a researcher belonging to Research Cloud RCn., r: role, p: permission)

Step 1: User R_{nx} created in under RCn

Step 2: home directory /password/profile set for R_{nx} in RCn

Step 3: If $n \cap x = 1$ then R_{nx} is a research cloud user.

Step 4: Profile of R_{nx} is synced with AAS user profile.

Step 5: Set home directory/profile for R_{nx} in RCx

Step 6: R_{nx}.r.RCn → R_{nx}.p.RCx

Step 7: R_{nx}.r.RCn→ R_{nx}.r.RCx

Step 8: R_{nx}.r. RCn ≥ R_{nx}.r. RCx

Step 9: R_{nx}.p. RCn = R_{nx}.p. RCx

Step 10: Else R_{nx} is not research user

Step 11: No sync with AAS.

4.6.2 Algorithm for Resource Allocation in CRC

In a PVC there are multiple Research Owners(RO). Each owner is allocated with certain resources to allocate to number of RCUs they create. When a researcher accesses the PVC, request the RO for the resources depending on the need of requirement RO assigns the resources to RCU. Resource demands of researchers differs depending on the analysis tools as well as iterations done. Researcher perform numerous iterations with multiple data sets, varying the parameters. Due to voluminous iterations, compute intensive performance analysis, and RCUs may runs out of memory and compute The proposed algorithm is designed for resource allocation according to the varying workload in CRC. But the resource utilization is not optimized and does not follow a comprehensive assessment strategy.

Algorithm 2: Resource allocation in CRC

Input

A: Maximum number of RCUs allocated for each researcher owner

N: Total number for RCUs available in CRC

B: Maximum number RCUs any researcher can request.

H: Maximum Resource set

P: Maximum resources set in PVC

X_i: RCU in use

Y_i: RCU Request in queue

i: RCU number.

j: resource allocated to the RCU.

Step 1: For $Y_i \neq 0$

If $X_i = 0$ then i=1 // creates first RCU

Else if

For i←0 to M, i= M-i

Step 2: For $Y_i \neq 0$ and $X_i = 0$

$X_i = X_1$

J← 0 to H

If $X_{ij} = X_{1j}$ // utilization reaches threshold

Then j++ →H

$X_{ij} \leq X_{1H}$

Step 3: For $Y_i \neq 0$ and $X_i \neq 0$

$X_i = X_{m-i}$

$J = H - j$

$X_{ij} \leftarrow X_{(M-i)(H-j)}$

If $X_{ij} = X_{(M-i)(H-j)}$ then

i++

j++

Step 4: For $Yi \neq 0$ and $X_i \neq 0$

$X_i = X_1$

$J{+}{+} \rightarrow H$

$X_{ij} \leq X_{1H}$

Step 5: if $B \leq A$ then

Get $RCU_{ij} (1 \leq B \leq A)$ from A

Create RCU_{ij}

Step 6: if $B > A$

$Y_i = 0 \quad X_{ij} > X_{AH}$ then

$A{+}{+} \rightarrow N$

$J{+}{+} \rightarrow P$

$X_{ij} \leq X_{NP}$

$X_{ij} = X_{NP}$

4.7 Evaluation of RCU Creation Time in CRC

Creation time indicates the speed and effectiveness of resource allocation in a virtualized environment. Table 4.3 shows the test results for RCU creation time in proposed framework with hybrid access control model. The resource allocation algorithm is implemented in Python 2.7. In same experimental setup, the time taken to create Virtual Machine, is as given in Table 4.4. Four iterations were conducted by changing the number of users. RCU and VM creation time calculated during each iteration for configurations ,2- core, 4GB RAM, 3- core,6 GB RAM, 4- core,8 GB

RAM. In each iteration the workload of system increased as the numbers users and size of the VM/RCU increased.

4.7.1 Experimental Setup

Four compute nodes with processor 5287U- i5 with 3 MB cache and 2.9 GHz. 2-core and 4 threads, 256 GB RAM connected using Layer -2 CISCO SF 300 switch. The systems are installed with Ubuntu 14.04 and Open stack to set up the test bed.

4.7.2 Result Analysis

The results shown in Table 4.3 indicates the creation time of RCU of specified configuration with fixed number of users in each iterations. Keeping the number of users fixed, the RCU size is varied and evaluated the creation time. The results indicate the RCU creation time does not vary much with more numbers of users and proposed framework performs an efficient resource allocation. When number of users increased by 400%, the creation time increased 32%, which is negligible. Similarly, the creation time of VM also was evaluated. The results of VM creation time is as shown in Table 4.4. In case of VM with 400% increase in number of users, the creation time increased by 58%.

Table 4. 3: Test Results for RCU Creation Time

No of users	Time in secs to create RCU		
	2 Core/4 GB RAM	3 Core/6 GB RAM	4 Core/8 GB RAM
5 Users	16	16	17
10 Users	17	17	17
15 Users	22	23	25
20 Users	22	24	25

Table 4. 4: Test Results for VM Creation Time

No of users	Time in secs to create VM		
	2 Core/4 GB RAM	3 Core/6 GB RAM	4 Core/8 GB RAM
5 Users	19	20	22
10 Users	19	20	24
15 Users	23	25	30
20 Users	25	25	30

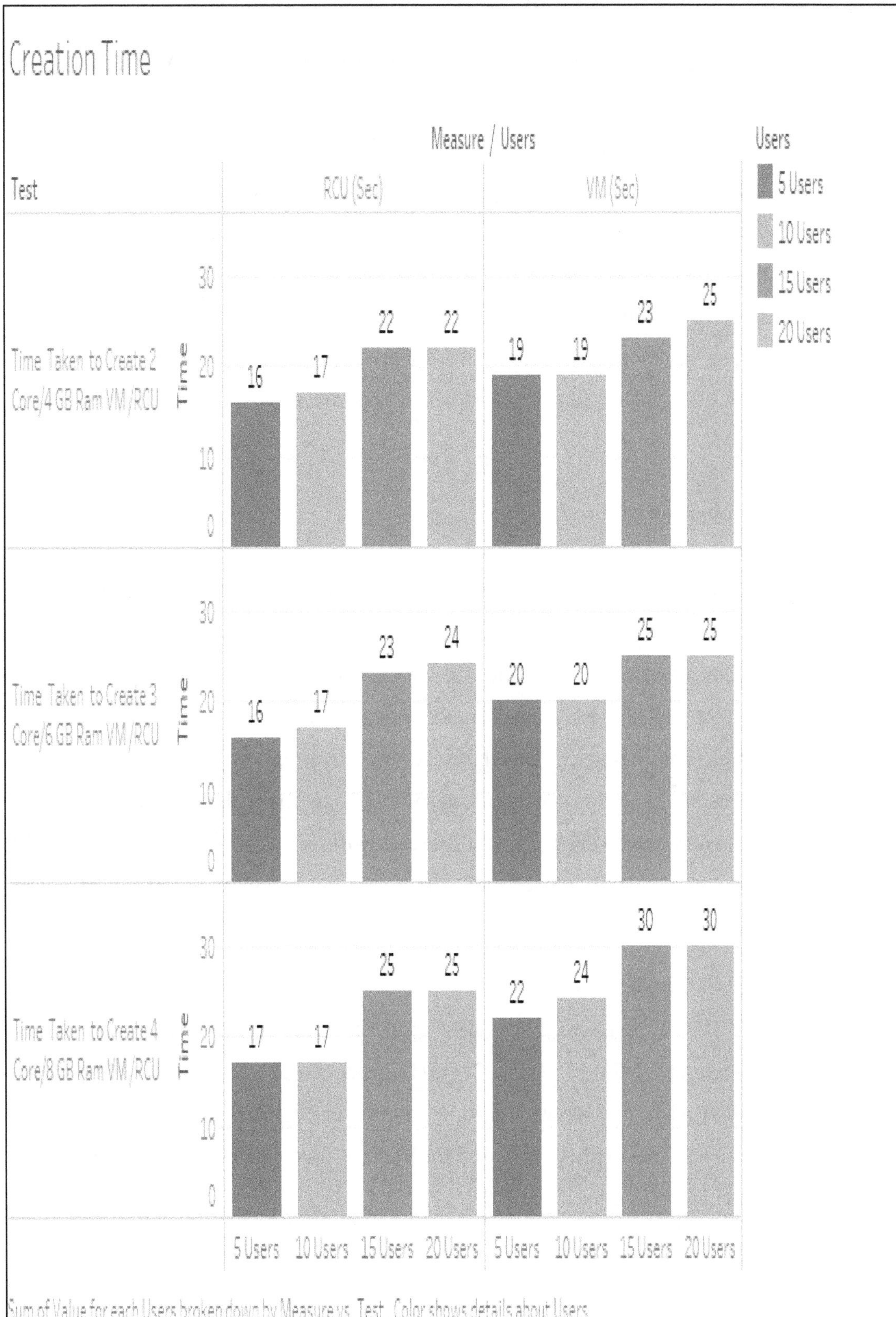

Figure 4. 3: Comparison of Creation Time for RCU and VM

4.7.3 Comparative Analysis of Creation Time of RCU with VM

Comparative analysis of RCU and VM creation time shown in Figure 4.3 demonstrates that creation time of RCU faster than that of VM which proves that resource allocation is faster in CRC with RCU. Even though containers have faster creation time than VMs due to less overheads, it is further enhanced due to the proposed algorithm. Even with more number of users demanding for resources, efficiency of resource allocation of CRC is better. The average creation time of RCU based CRC is 22% higher the VM based systems.

4.8 Evaluation of Finish Time

Efficiency of RCU-based CRC and VM based systems were evaluated with reference to the finish time. The improvement in finish time indicates increased efficiency of resource allocation in CRC. The finish time was evaluated for VM based systems and RCU based CRC systems by running a .net application and sagemath computations. sagemath is open source mathematics software. The computationally light .net application and sage math computations chosen and multiple iterations were done for different configurational setups of VM and RCU. The resource allocation algorithm proposed is implemented in Python 2.7.

4.8.1 Experimental Setup

The experimental test bed consists of four physical machines with configuration 5287U (core i5), 2.9 GHz processor ,2-core, 4 threads,3 MB cache, 4.00 GB RAM, 1GB network card, 24 port layer 2 CISCO switch (SF 300). Ubuntu 14.04, Open stack with LXD used for RCU. Windows 2012 server Standard edition with service pack 2 used for VM.

4.8.2 Result Analysis

Fifty iterations were conducted for computationally lighter .net application and ten iterations for Sage math computations. Table 4.5 shows average finish time for execution of a .net application for configuration -1 with 2-core processor and

RAM 1GB and configuration- 2 with 4-core compute, 8 GB RAM. Table 4.6 shows the average finish time calculated for execution of sage math computation for configuration - 3 with 6-core compute, RAM 8 GB and configuration -4 with 8-core compute, RAM 16 GB.

Table 4. 5: Average finish time for executing a .net application

Configurations	Average finish time with .net application in secs	
	VM	**RCU**
2 Core/1 GB RAM	83.06	45.18
4 Core/8 GB RAM	82.7	38.14

Table 4. 6: Average finish time for executing a sagemath application

Configurations	Average finish time with sagemath in secs	
	VM	**RCU**
6 Core/8 GB RAM	1839.56	1086.33
8 Core/16 GB RAM	1839	952

The finish time evaluated for executing a .net application in 2 core /1 GB RAM configuration of RCU and VM is demonstrated in Figure 4.4. Average finish time variation for RCU is less than 5% and VM is less than 10%, which indicates the both RCU and VM has stability in performance which is very important in collaborative research environments. The average finish time evaluated with .net application for VM is 83.06 secs and RCU is 45.18 secs.

Similarly, the finish time was evaluated for 4 core /8 GB RAM configuration of RCU and VM and is represented graphically in Figure 4.5. Average finish time variation for RCU is less than 3% and VM is less than 8%. The average finish time evaluated with .net application for VM is 82.7 secs and RCU is 38.14 secs.

Figure 4.6 represents the finish Time for sage math application in 4 core /8 GB RAM configuration RCU/VM. Average finish time variation for RCU is less than 1% and

VM is less than 8%. The average finish time evaluated with .net application for VM is 1839.56 secs and RCU is 1086.33 secs.

Figure 4.7 represents the finish time for sage math application in 8 core /16 GB RAM configuration RCU/VM. Average finish time variation for RCU is less than 1% and VM is 8%. The average finish time evaluated with sage math computations for VM is 1839 secs and RCU is 952 secs. The results of the experiments implies that RCU based CRC effectively utilizes the resources and has a reduced finish time even with resource intensive applications like sage math.

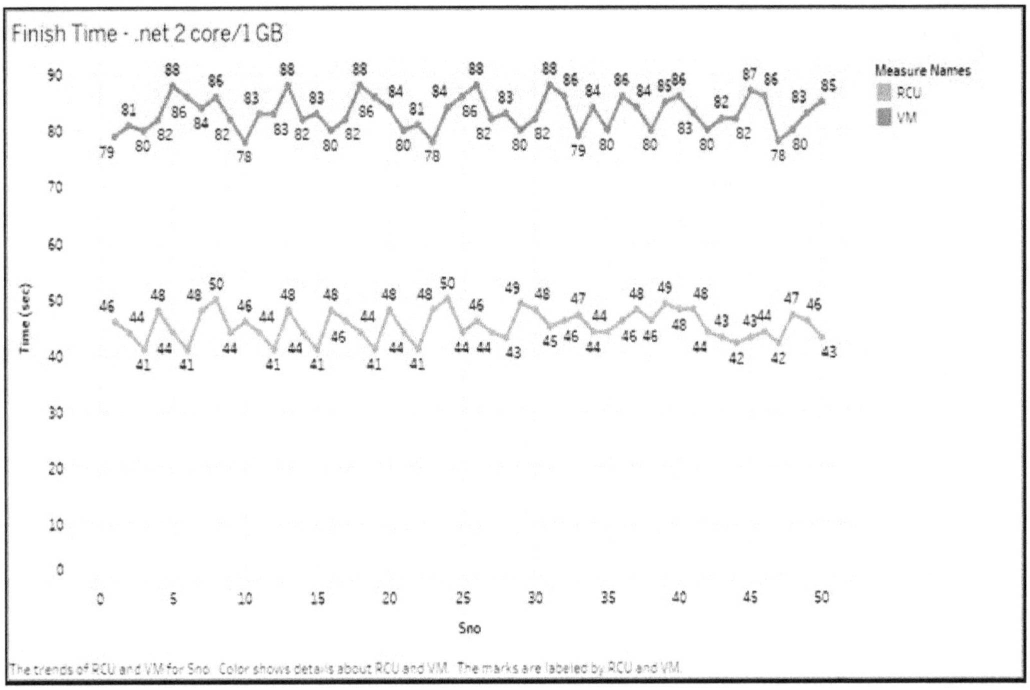

Figure 4.4: Finish Time for .net application in Configuration-1

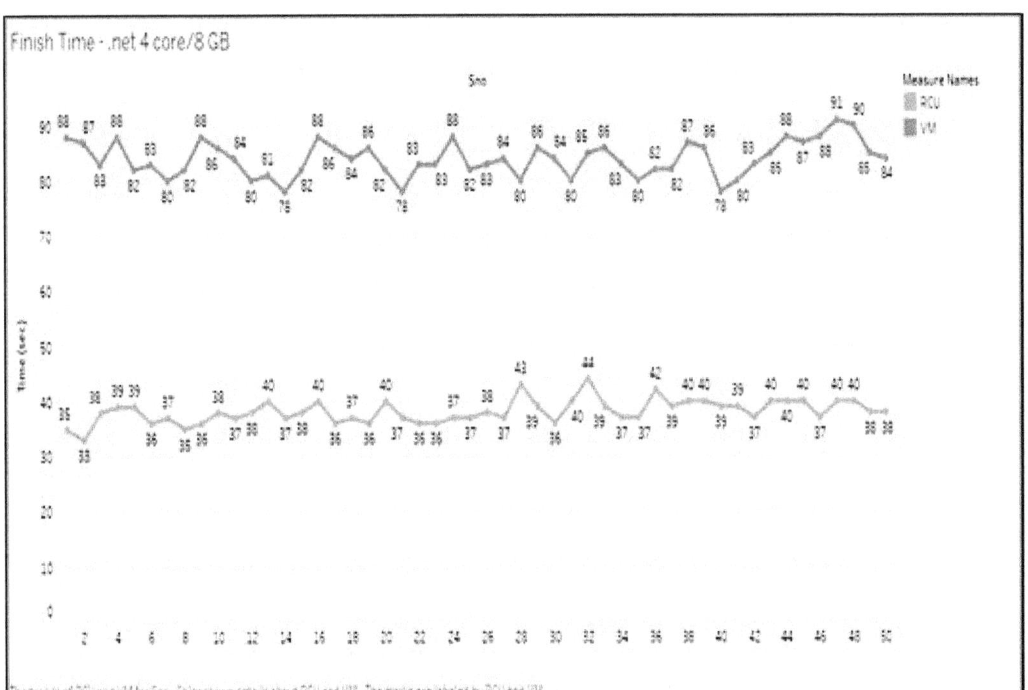

Figure 4.5: Finish Time for .net application in Configuration-2

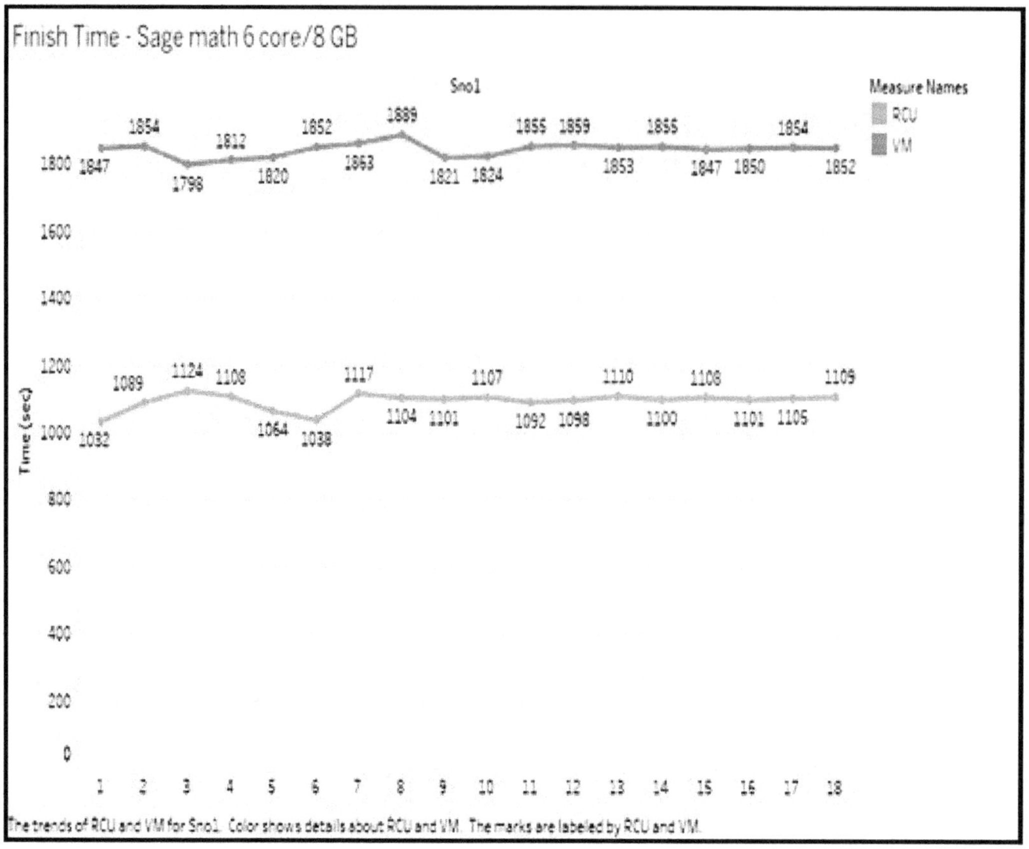

Figure 4.6: Finish Time for sage math application in Configuration-3

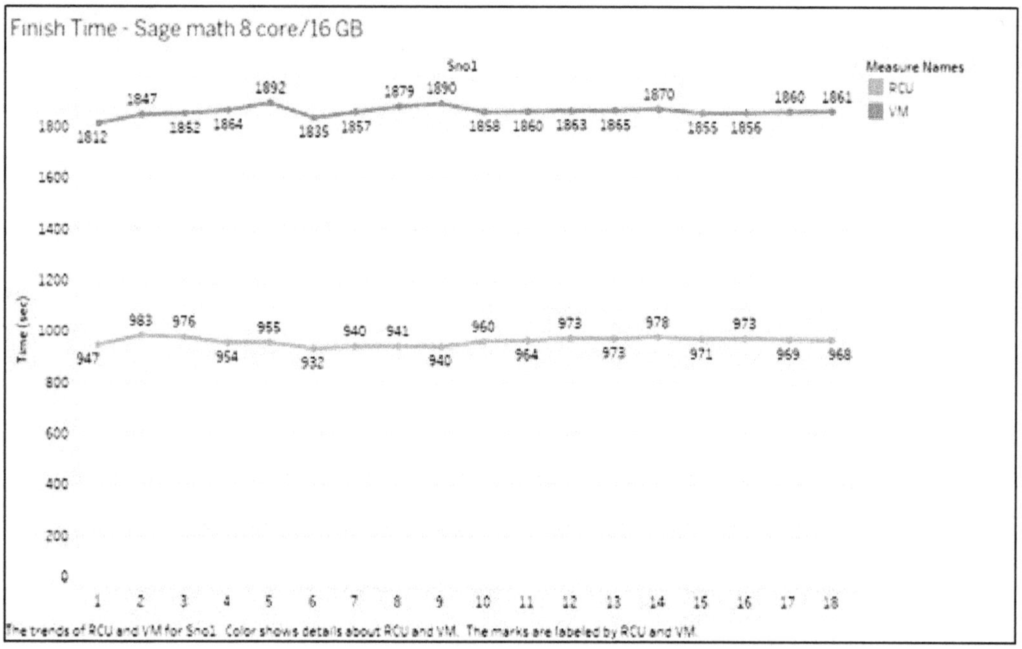

Figure 4.7: Finish Time for sage math application in Configuration-4

4.8.3 Comparative analysis

The comparison of data in Table 4.5 and Table 4.6 indicates that RCU based systems delivered a finish time that is higher by 45%, 53.8 %, 48%, 41% than VM based systems using configuration-1, configuration-2, configuration-3 and configuration-4 respectively.

The comparative analysis represented graphically in Figure 4.8 and Figure 4.9 shows that with more of resources available, CRC could deliver improved finish time than Virtual Machines because of better utilization of available resources employed by means of the proposed algorithm.

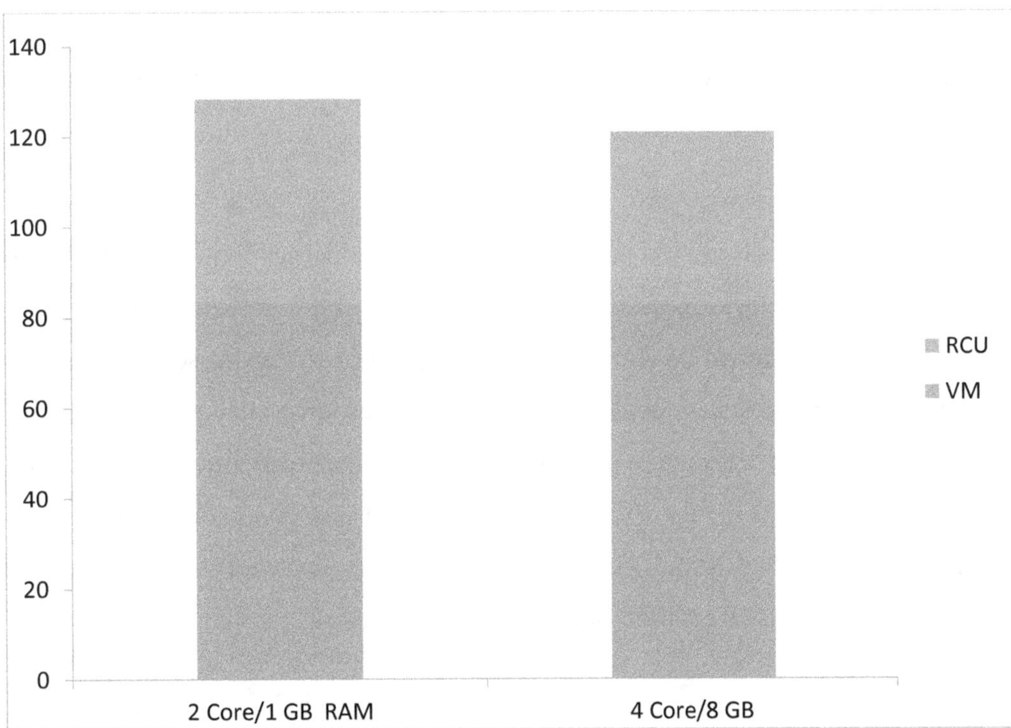

Figure 4. 8: Comparison of average finish time for .net application

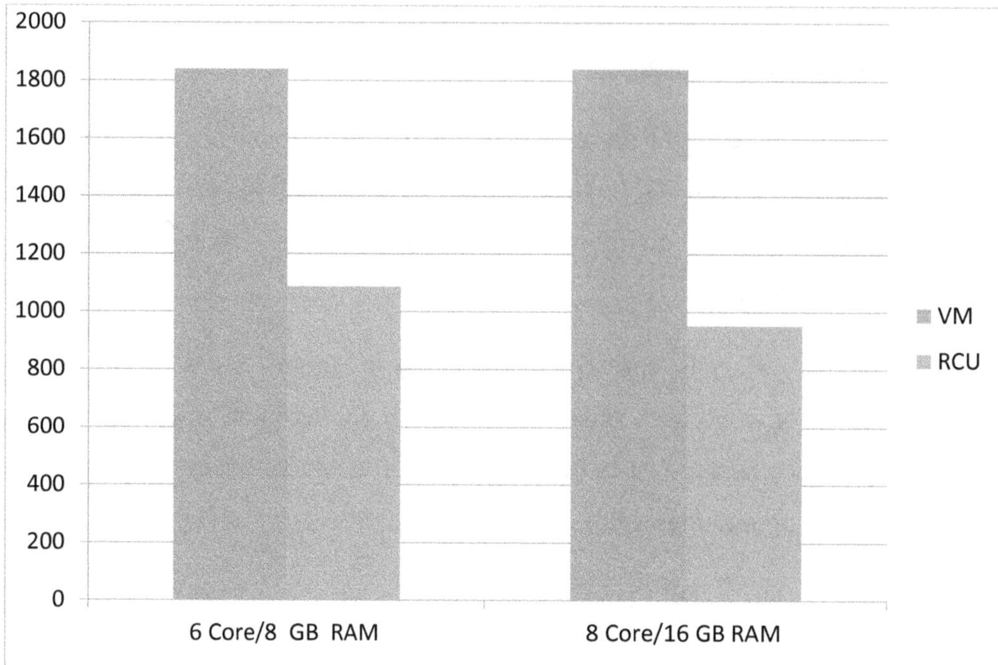

Figure 4. 9: Comparison of average finish time for sagemath computation

4.9 Summary

A detail discussion on the proposed authentication and authorisation framework and hybrid access control model is presented in the chapter. The novel algorithm for user creation and login based on trust model addresses the concerns in authentication and access control. The proposed resource allocation algorithm has improved resource efficiency of CRC. The chapter has elaborated a detail analysis of results obtained for the experiments conducted and comparative analysis with existing approaches using Virtual Machines, to evaluate efficiency in resource utilization in terms of creation time and finish time.

CHAPTER 5

CHAPTER-5

AN APPROACH FOR OPTIMIZING THE DYNAMIC RESOURCE PROVISIONING IN COLLABORATIVE RESEARCH CLOUD

5.1 Preface

This chapter will discuss the need for dynamic resource provisioning in collaborative research cloud and the proposed system model to optimize resource utilization. The chapter will also explain how the proposed CRC framework addresses the challenges in provisioning of resources, dynamically as per the varying workloads of applications and analysis tools that are significantly resource-hungry. The proposed approach employs on demand and custom-built containerization, comprehensively assessing the resource requirements in order to accomplish optimum resource utilization in collaborative research environment. The proposed algorithms aim to resolve the dynamic resource allocation problem and aims to reduce finish time, increase the throughput of entire system and attain optimal resource utilization, making use of the unused residual resources.

5.2 Research Problem

Dynamically allocating the resources to meet up with the inconsistent demands of resource hungry applications utilized in research scenario is a major problem in collaborative research environments. Collaborative scientific research comprises researchers in divergent disciplines from many organizations, associating to perform analysis, scientific trials or simulations that may be data, compute and resource exhaustive and often with erratic requests for resources. Such applications or research tools needs extremely dynamic resource allocation approach and also endure bursty workloads. But, existing platforms for collaborative research hinge on the Cloud Services Provider (CSP) for resource provisioning that follows static provisioning methods and independent scheduling of the applications. Dearth of approaches for comprehensively assessing the applications and the total obtainable resources bring about over- utilization or under –utilization and hence with increased time for running an application.

Hence, the key problems noticed with respect to dynamic provisioning resources in collaborative research cloud platforms are as follows:

Variable workloads: Resource utilization in collaborative research platforms can differ based on analysis tools. Researcher performs many iterations on same data set with different parameters. The fixed amount of resources allocated may not adequate for multiple reruns of experiments performed using diverse datasets.

Bursty workloads: Data and compute-intensive tools and applications create bursty workloads. The ephemeral workloads that varies with time generates high demand for resources and is very common in final stages scientific analysis. In [37] has illustrated a scenario of such bursty workloads generated when with the analysis tool Parallel ROOT Facility (PROOF) [4] used in High Energy Physics (HEP).

Resource locking: Resource provisioning in accordance with the spontaneous workloads which arises while running scientific and analysis tools necessitates the removal of resource locking owing to fixed provisioning of the resources. Furthermore, such provisioning strategies leads to under-utilization or over-utilization that positions a major concern in resource utilization.

Lack of comprehensive resource assessment: Increased application execution time results from lack strategies for comprehensively assessing the applications and the available resources. Lack of adoption of a complete assessment scheme leads to lower resource utilization and therefore increases the execution time and have an effect on the finish time and also the throughput of the entire system.

5.3 Research methodolgy

To address the resource allocation problem in CRC, a system model was designed by organizing the functionalities of entire framework into different layers. A virtual infrastructure of the framework was conceptualized. Through optimization of the resource utilization, the dynamic resource provisioning problem is addressed. This approach minimizes the finish time and improve the throughput. The proposed algorithms for resource allocation enhanced the adhoc scalability of CRC by commissioning unutilized residual resources and henceforth minimized the finish time for running a tool or an application.

The proposed approach weights on containerization, comprehensively assessing of the resource requirements and accomplishes optimal resource utilization in collaborative research environments. The proposed algorithm utilizes under-utilized residual resources to improve the finish time and better utilization of resources the model utilizes the unutilized resources allocated to RCU and PVC. The resources include compute, memory, storage and bandwidth.

5.3.1 System Model

The key functional components of CRC are organized as layered architecture that consist of Physical layer, Service layer, Virtualization and Control layer, Delivery layer. Figure 5.1 demonstrates the proposed layered architecture of CRC framework.

Physical layer assigns required processing power, bandwidth and storage that builds the resource stack of an RCU. Virtualization and Control layer is implemented through OS level virtualization to decreases the system overheads in comparison to the Virtual Machine based technology. This layer based on container based virtualization delivers sufficient abstraction for each researcher and assures isolation of for the resources. Service layer serves as a repository to stores RCU instances in OVF (Open Virtual Format). OVF format improves the portability and platform independence of RCU. The researchers access the assigned RCU through the service layer. Delivery layer uses rapid, scalable containerization to accommodate varying resource requests in CRC.

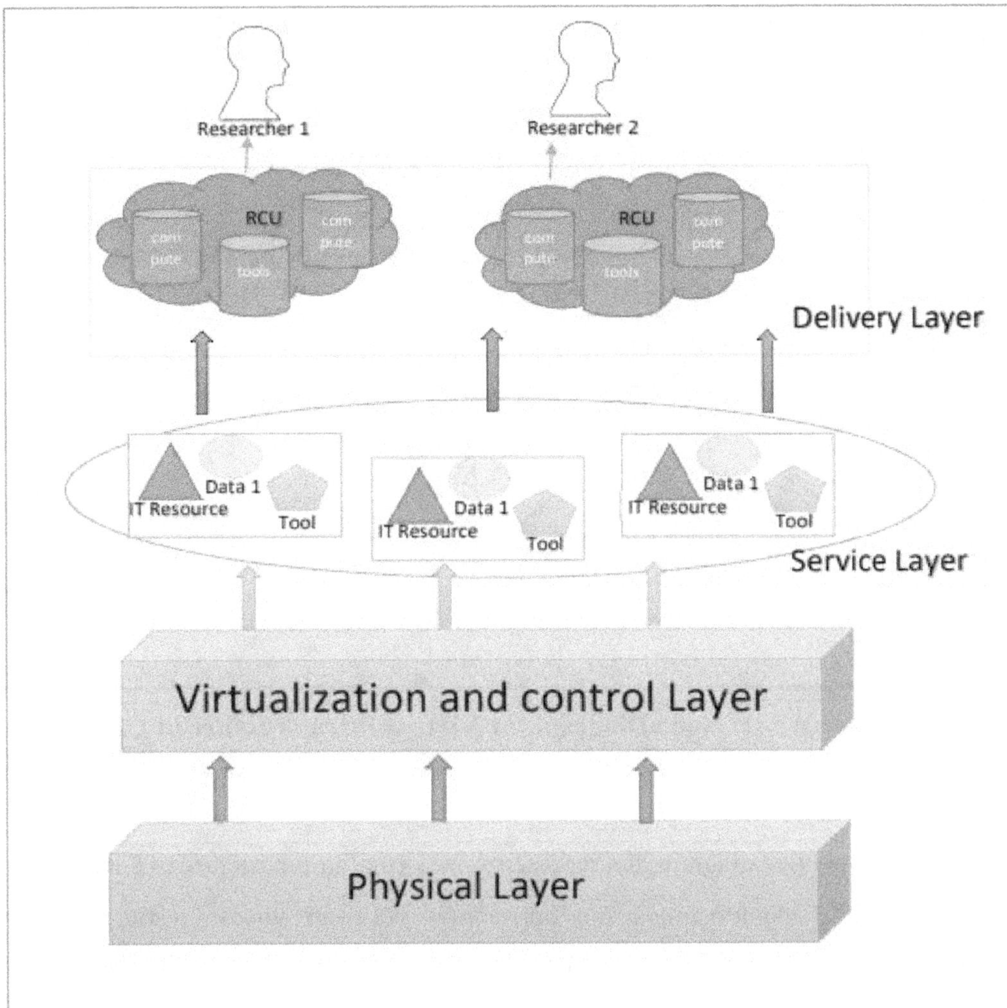

Figure 5. 1: Layered Architecture of CRC.

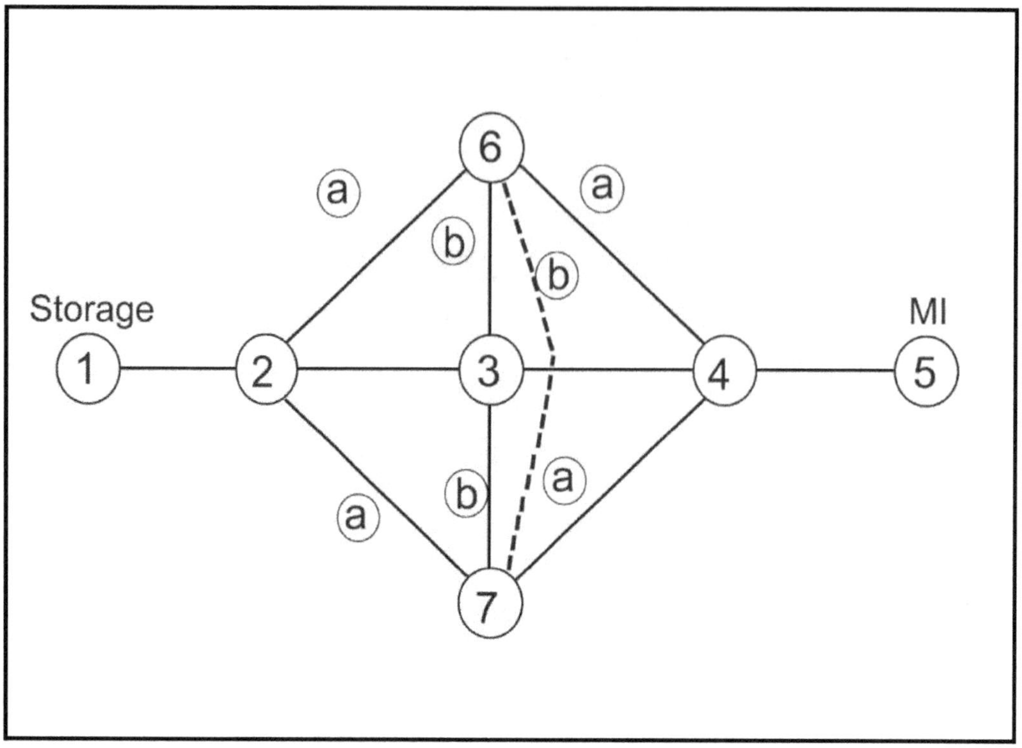

Figure 5. 2: Node Diagram for Virtual Infrastructure of CRC

The proposed node diagram that represents the virtual infrastructure of CRC depicted in Figure 5.2 demonstrates the correlation between virtual resources of the framework. Multiple virtual resources are connected through virtual routers. The specified virtual path depends on the allocated bandwidth.

Assumptions:

- **a** is the virtual link bandwidth among compute resources and routers.
- **b** is the virtual limit latency between the nodes.

Management Interface associates the available resources using virtual routers. MI chooses one of the compute nodes (3, 6, 7) depending on the job. The routes created with virtual router 4 are 5-4-6, 5-4-7 , 5-4-3. The node numbers 3, 6, 7 are linked to storage node 1 by means of virtual router 2. The comprehensive assessment of the resources available in CRC and allocation of required bandwidth, resources for RCU is accomplished through MI. Table 5.1 demonstrates the purpose of individual nodes of Virtual Infrastructure diagram.

Table 5. 1: Node functions

Node	Purpose
1	Storage
2 ,4	Routers (virtual)
3,6,7	compute
5	MI

5.3.2 Mathematical Modelling

Let Np be the total available resources (memory, compute, bandwidth, storage,) in CRC. **r** denotes RCU and residual resources available in an RCU is represented $\boldsymbol{b_r^p}$. **a** denotes bandwidth of RCU and **b** denotes the latency between RCUs.

For an application or job $\mathbf{A_j}$ having workload $\mathbf{L_j}$, and maximum acceptable service delay is denoted as T_j .The minimal resource requirement $\boldsymbol{R_j^u}$ is for a job A_j having workload $\mathbf{L_j}$ calculated as

$$R_j^u = \frac{L_j}{T_j} \qquad (1)$$

If the job size is lesser than a definite minimal value, it will not be taken for consideration in order to avoid underutilization and hence the resource locking.

Minimum size of job size should be $\geq Lj\ \beta_j$ where $\beta_j = \dfrac{\text{smallest workload}}{Lj}$

The smallest workload is defined an atomic workload that can be executed by any compute device. The proposed model considers the significance of smallest workload and minimal job size, as it helps to avoid resource locking and underutilization. The total residual resources available in CRC is calculated as part of comprehensive assessment strategy adopted by MI.

Aggregate residual resources in CRC, **Z** is estimated as,

$$\sum_{r}^{N^p} b_r^p \qquad (2)$$

Finish time of a job or an application is defined as the ratio of workload to resource requirements with a definite time delay. Finish time is minimized when residual resources are optimally utilization.

Finish time F_j^T for an application or Job A_j is calculated as,

$$F_j^T = \frac{A_j}{R_j^u} - \frac{A_j}{(\frac{Z}{T_j})} \qquad (3)$$

Let Z_r is assigned bandwidth for a researcher, unutilized bandwidth in a RCU is denoted as U, the maximal number of RCUs which can be generated in CRC is represented as **n** and number of active RCUs at any moment of time is denoted by **x**.

Maximum throughput allotted to a RCU (X_r) is computed as:

$$X_r = Z_r + \sum_{n-r}^{n} U \qquad (4)$$

The overall throughput of CRC is evaluated as

$$\sum_{1}^{x} a - \sum_{1}^{x-1} b \qquad (5)$$

Optimal resource required for job $O_j^u = \frac{L_j}{T_j} + Z \qquad (6)$

5.3.3 Algorithmic Implementation

An ad hoc, dynamic resource provisioning calls for an approach that wholly asses the resource demands of the users of CRC and total resources available in the research cloud framework. The algorithm proposed for dynamic resource provisioning minimized the finish time which in turn increases the throughput of CRC and accomplishes optimal resource utilization. If the initial provisioned RCU resources are not sufficient to serve the resource requirements of an application, residual resources of other RCUs of CRC are assigned dynamically.

Algorithm 1: Algorithm for dynamic resource provisioning

Input:

N^P: Total Available resources in CRC

r: RCU number

A_j: Job/Application

L_j: Work Load

T_j: Maximum allowed time delay

M_p^j : Minimal resource required to complete a smallest workload

I: maximum idle time for a RCU

$R_j^{u_i}$:Minimal resources required for job

Z: Total Residual resource of CRC

Output: F_j^t , X_r

Step 1: Job /workload requested

Step 2: Create RCU, r

Step 3: Resource allocated to RCU r $\leftarrow R_j^u$ $(R_j^u > M_j^P)$

Step 4 : Finish Time F_j^T = $A_j \div R_j^u$

Step 5: Check whether finish time > T_j then go to step 7 else go to step 9

Step 7: Residual resource added to RCU r = R_j^u +Z

Step 8: Throughput, $X_r = Z_r + \sum_{n-r}^{n} Y$

Step 9: Finish time , $F_j^T = \frac{l_j}{R_j^u} - \frac{l_j}{(\frac{Z}{T_j})}$

Step 10:Check whether $O_j^u > R_j^u$ then go to step 7

Step 11: If idle time of RCU ≥I

Step 12: RCU decommissioned

Step 13: R_j^u=0

5.4 Evaluation of Finish time for Compute Intensive Applications with Utilization of Residual Resources

Lower resource utilization in cloud environments arises due to lack of methods to comprehensively assess the resources available and demand for resources. Inefficiency of resource utilization leads to increased execution time and affects the finish time.

Finish time evaluated by differing the residual resources of VM, native LXD, and RCU to execute computation intensive sagemath functions. The functions for integer factorization, factorial and Bernoulli number were executed in sagemath software. The computational function for Bernoulli number is resource exhaustive while integer factorization, factorial functions are not.

Three iterations were done for evaluation of finish time for RCU, LXD , VM systems with same configuration of 8-core and 16 GB RAM was conducted in three iterations changing the residual resources. In the first iteration residual resources made available in the system was 0%, 25% residual resources for second iteration available, and during the third iteration with procurable residual resources of 60%. The efficiency of resource optimization with regard to finish time was evaluated by differing the amount of available residual resources.

5.4.1 Result Analysis

The results in Table 5.2 indicates that the finish time remains the same even with increase in residual resources available, for executing all the three applications in case of VM and LXD. However, RCU showed a sweeping improvement in finish time with availability of residual resources.

Table 5. 2: Evaluation of Finish time with residual resources

sagemath functions	Residual resource (%)	Finish Time (secs)		
		VM	LXD	RCU
Bernoulli number	0	248	221	221
	25	248	221	177
	60	248	221	160
Integer factorisation	0	170	155	150
	25	170	155	134
	60	170	155	113
Factorial	0	39	32	32
	25	39	32	24
	60	39	32	13

5.4.2 Comparative Analysis

The comparative analysis shown in Figures 5.3, 5.4, 5.5 proves that even with the available residual resources the finish time of VM and native LXD has no variation, but RCU efficiently consumed residual resources and therefore a better finish time.

Figure 5.3 indicates that for Bernoulli number computations RCU has 10.8% improved finish time compared to VM, with 0% residual resources and RCU and LXD has almost same finish time. With 25% residual resources RCU finish time is 28.6% better than VM and 19.9 % than LXD. RCU finish time is 35.5% better than VM and 27.6 % than LXD with 60% residual resources.

Figure 5.4 shows that with respect to integer factorisation calculation RCU has 15.2% better finish time than VM and 3.2 % better finish time than LXD with no residual resources. With 25% residual resources RCU finish time is 21.1% better than VM and 13.5 % than LXD. RCU finish time is 33.5% better than VM and 27.1 % than LXD in case of 60 % residual resource availability.

Figure 5.5 shows that factorial calculation RCU has 17.9% better finish time than VM and same performance compared to LXD with no residual resources. With 25%residual resources RCU finish time is 38.4% better than VM and 25% than

LXD. RCU finish time is 66.6 %better than VM and 59.3% than LXD in case of 60 % residual resource availability. Hence, the proposed CRC framework effectively used the unutilized residual resources, attained faster finish time and a better resource efficiency.

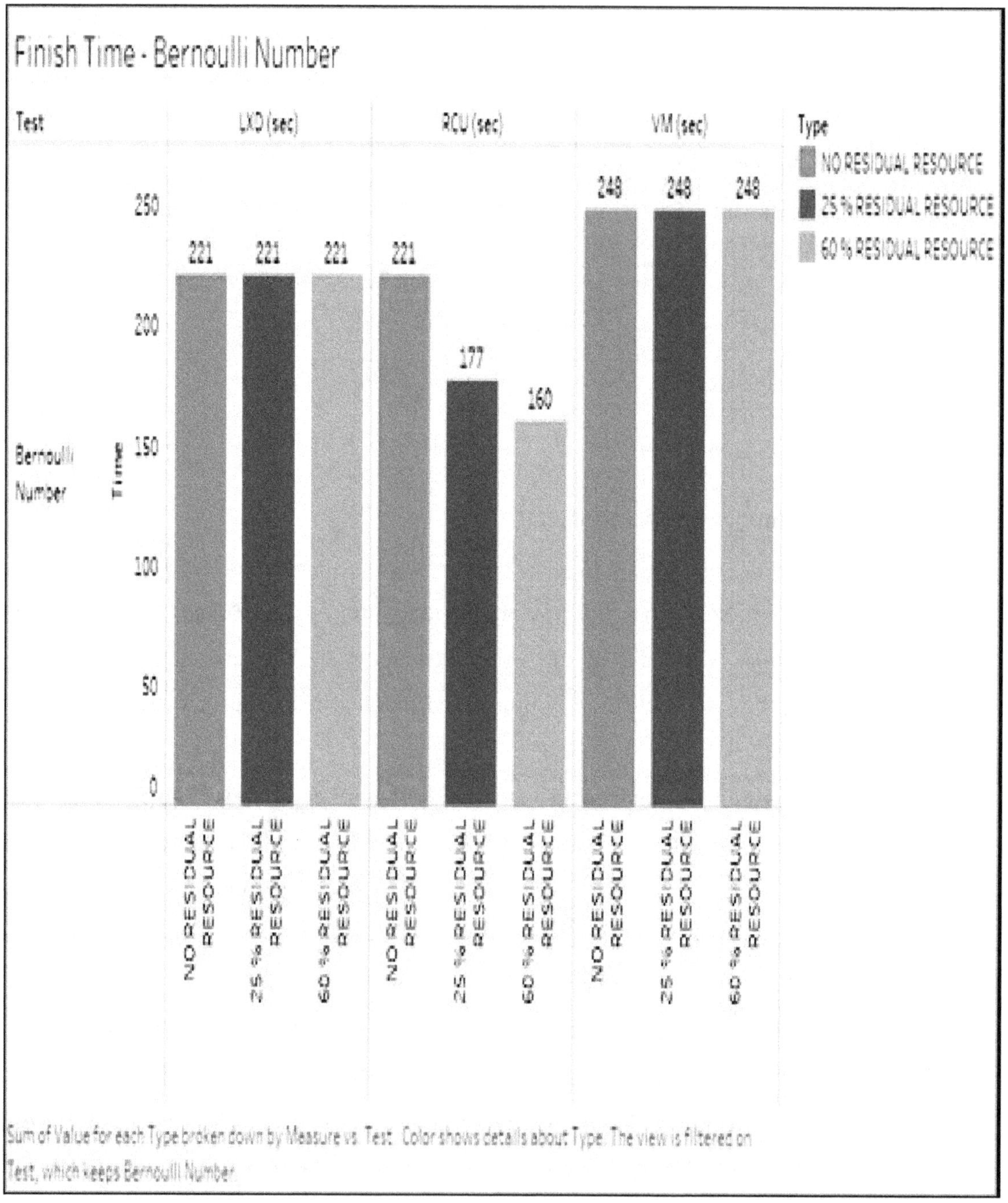

Figure 5. 3: Comparison of Finish Time for Bernoulli Number

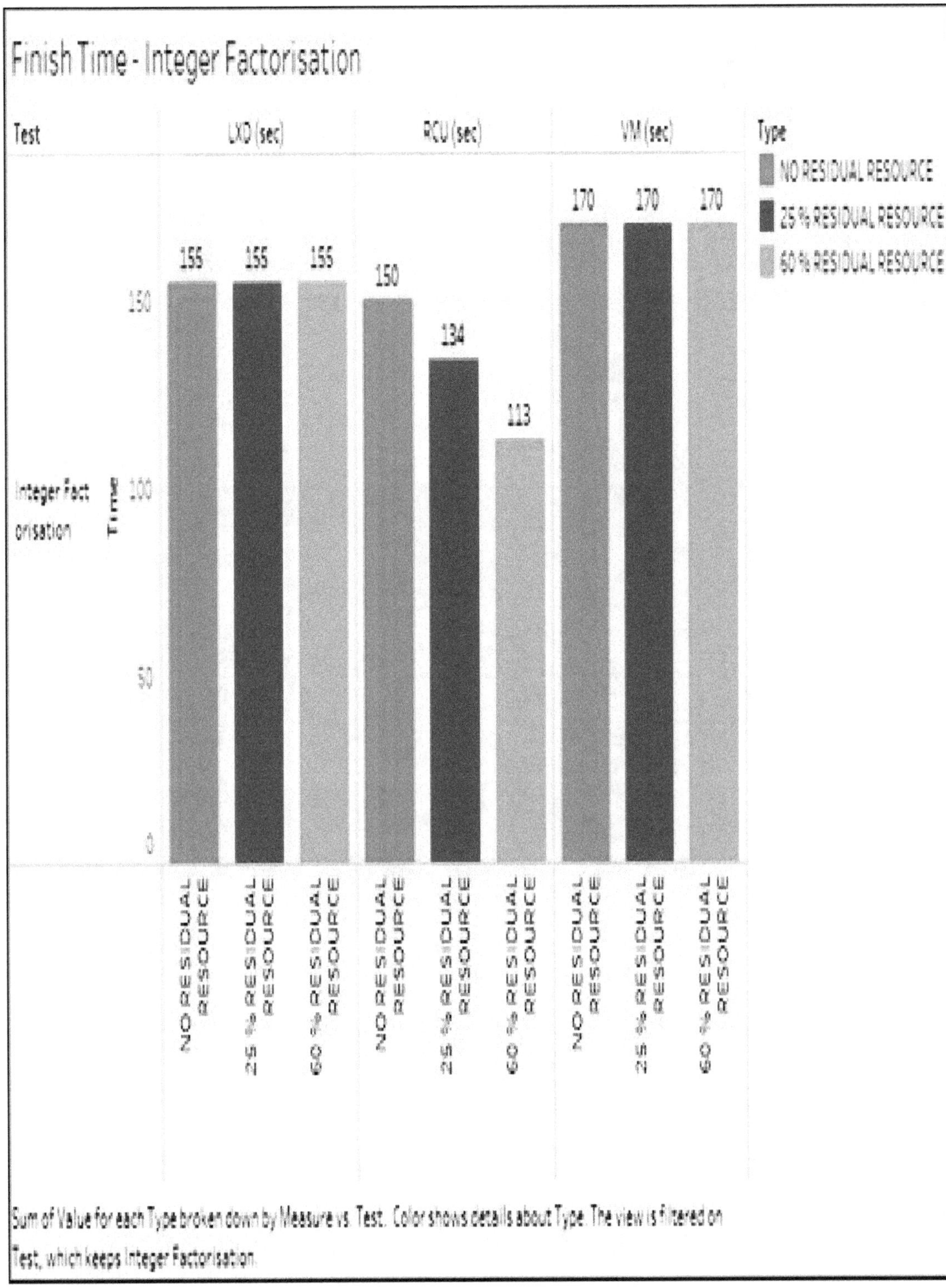

Figure 5. 4: Comparison of Finish Time for Integer Factorisation

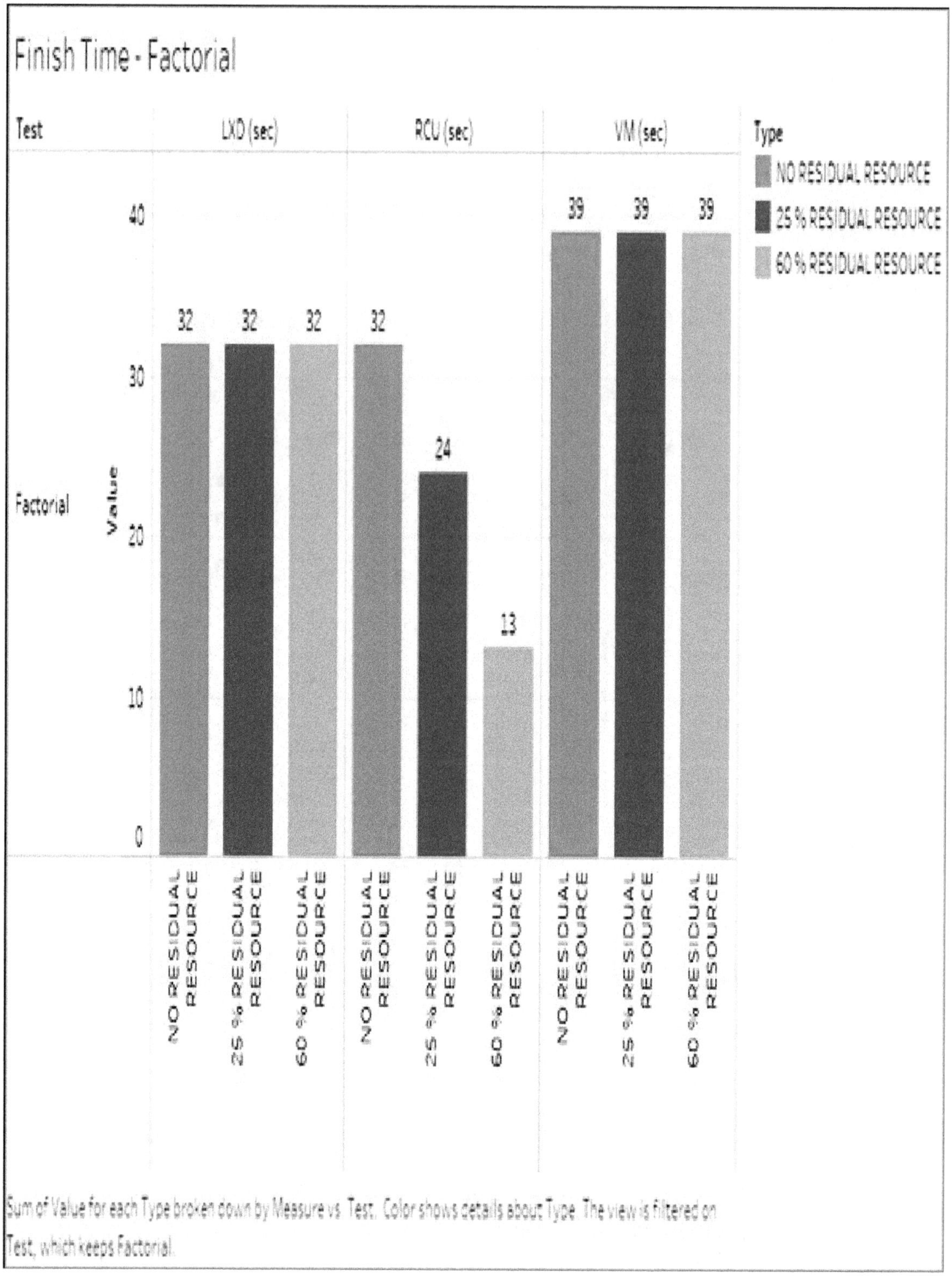

Figure 5. 5: Comparison of Finish Time for Factorial Function

5.5 Evaluation of Throughput for Variable Data Sizes

Experiments were conducted to estimate the throughput of CRC and VM based systems, while processing data of different sizes. Ten iterations were conducted, with configuration 2-core/ 4GB RAM / 500GB hard disk for processing 1 GB and 4 GB data and 8-core/16GB RAM/500 GB hard disk for processing data larger than 100 GB. The result analysis intends to study the effectiveness of RCU to achieve improved throughput through utilization of the idle bandwidth.

5.5.1 Result `Analysis

The throughput for VM based systems are given in Table 5.3 and the throughput for RCU based CRC are given in Table 5.4. The amount of data transferred is a major bottleneck in collaborative research cloud environment. The values in Table 5.3 and Table 5.4 indicates that VM machine shows a reduced throughput with increased data size even with more resources available but RCU based CRC has an improvement in throughput with increase in data sizes and resources.

Table 5. 3: Throughput of VM based systems

System configuration	Data (GB)	Number of iterations	Throughput (Gbps)
2-core /4GB RAM /500GB hard disk	1	10	149.4
2-core /4GB RAM /500GB hard disk	4	10	140.5
8-core /16GB RAM /500 GB hard disk	100	10	139.3

Table 5. 4: Throughput for RCU based CRC

System configuration	Data (GB)	Number of iterations	Throughput (Gbps)
2-core /4GB RAM /500GB hard disk	1	10	169.2
2-core /4GB RAM /500GB hard disk	4	10	174.7
8-core /16GB RAM /500 GB hard disk	100	10	181.3

5.5.2 Comparative Analysis

It is very clearly evident from Figure 5.6 that RCU based CRC achieves an better throughput of 13% higher than the throughput of VM based systems for the processing of 1GB data . An increase in throughput of 24% , 30.15% was observed for processing 4GB and 100 GB data respectively.Therefore RCU succeeds to attain a enhanced throughput with employment of unused bandwidth . The above analysis infers that RCU based CRC is suitable for collaborative research platforms which often involves bulk data migrations and exchange of bigger datasets .

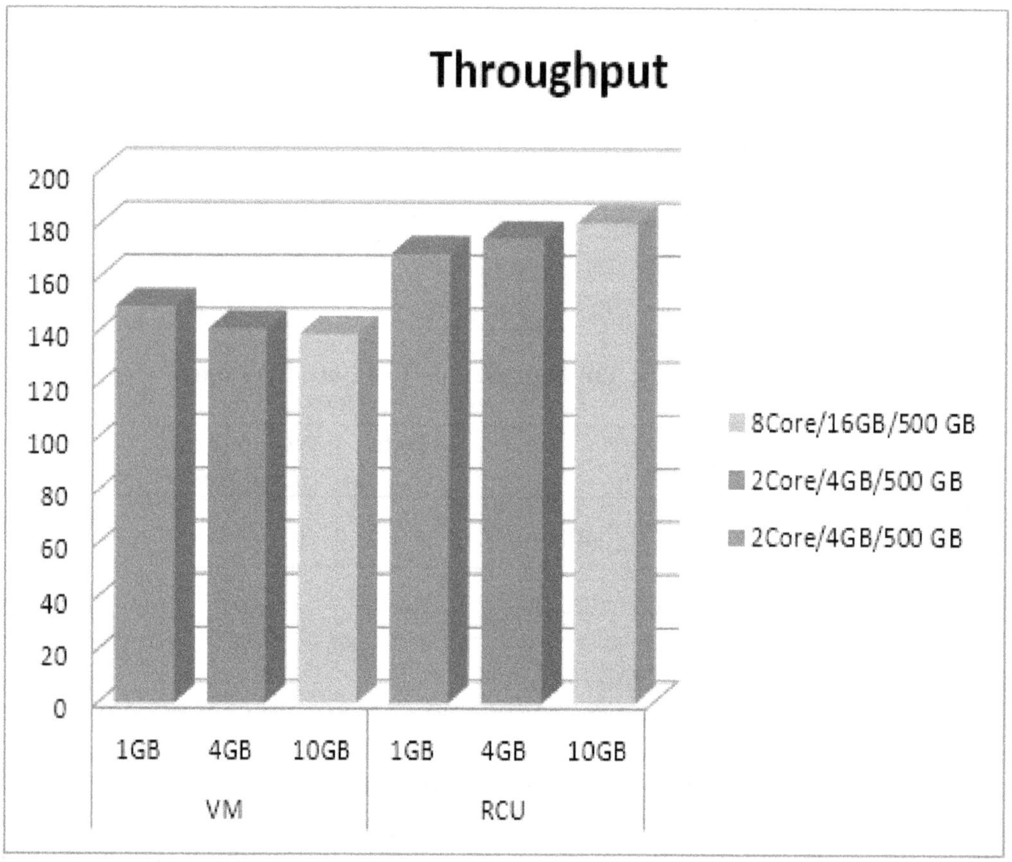

Figure 5. 6: Comparative Analysis of Throughput of CRC

5.6 Summary

The chapter has elucidated how the proposed CRC framework, dynamically provisions the resources corresponding to the workloads of applications or analysis tools. The proposed methodology comprehensively assesses the resource demands in CRC as well as total available residual resources in the system. The proposed algorithms intend to decrease finish time for application execution and increase throughput for optimizing the resource utilization.

CHAPTER 6

CHAPTER-6

SECURITY AND ISOLATION IN COLLABORATIVE RESEARCH CLOUD

6.1 Preface

This chapter will discuss the security vulnerabilities of cloud environments, security requirements in collaborative research cloud and will elaborate the proposed approach towards the augmentation of access model to increase the security and isolation of the shared resources in CRC. A novel algorithm proposed for secured flow of information is also elaborated in this chapter. The chapter will explain exclusive analysis of data derived from the experiments conducted and benchmarking. The performance isolation benchmarking of collaborative research cloud framework, comparative analysis with existing approaches using VM and LXD are also discussed this chapter.

6.2 Problem Identification

Research institutions nowadays leverage on cloud services for collaborative efforts and to make the research data, results and tools used for visualization of results accessible to the researchers as an alternative to discrete data management and sharing frameworks. However, there are numerous challenges with respect to security and confidentiality of sensitive research data and applications, shared among researchers. Common security vulnerabilities of cloud environments also add on to this problem.

- **Breach of privacy and confidentiality**: Preserving the security and confidentiality of sensitive research data and proprietary applications, when shared in a publically hosted collaborative cloud platform is an arduous challenge. Although approaches like k-anonymization [28] and differential privacy [2] were used to maintain confidentiality of data, they are not advantageous in collaborative research platforms where multiple researchers need to share the data and applications along with all its dependencies to foster reproducibility of research. With breach of confidentiality, the data owners lose trust in sharing sensitive data and tools with other researchers.

- **Lack of control on shared resources:** The breach of security and lack of control over the shared resources makes the researchers hesitant in sharing data, tools, and inferences with others. Cloud based reproducible research reduces the time and efforts required to replicate the computational environment used by the original researcher to perform an analysis using specific application or tool. Researchers may have varying sharing requirements, may be read or view of data, data fetch, fetch and run an application, or may need to reproduce a system environment to evaluate an experimental result. Several approaches have been proposed for sharing of applications or tools, data, along with complete compute environment among researchers. Workflow software, virtual machine and containers are deployed to for sharing of applications bundled with all its dependencies. But, when the proprietary tools and application get distributed to multiple researchers, the original research owner may lose control over the it. When a researcher (data owner) share the data and grant access privileges on the data to another researcher (data receiver), the receiver may redeploy the data to other researchers lacking the knowledge of the data owner. However, due to the breach of security and confidentiality of the sensitive research data, data owners are pessimistic in sharing data and tools with other researchers. The original researchers to whom the data, tools, and results belong to, are uncertain about the control over the resources that are distributed among multiple users in collaborative research environments. Though various solutions have been proposed in literatures, for example [46] [64], to address secure data sharing in collaborative research environments and data owners access control problem, much work does not exist on secured sharing and access control of application or tools.

- **Lack of a flexible, policy based access control**: The original researcher to whom the research resources belong to, should be able to define the user policy regarding access the data and applications and what are the permitted actions on the resources. The coarse grained access control models fail to deliver the passable flexibility that empowers the user to specify the access policies. Securely sharing the sensitive research data and applications across such public hosted collaboration platforms necessitate a strong access control approach that guarantees confidentiality and authorized access. Difficulty in distribution and revocation of encryptions keys and limited traceability due to mathematical inclination, makes encryption techniques less suitable for a securing the shared data and tools in collaborative research environments [64]. Customary access control mechanisms, which are largely role specific, imposes control over the data and tools, mostly in application or service perspective. Data owner does not have control over the shared data beyond policy enforcement points, and traditional access control methods are not sufficient to ensure its security [65].

- **General security challenges in cloud model**: In a multitenant cloud environment, virtualization enables users to share physical resources with others. but it also causes threat to the user's resources. Malicious virtual machines are easily vulnerable to hypervisor attacks. Side channel attacks are another persistent threat in virtualized systems sharing resources, where malicious code is injected to another virtual machine. Network virtualized clouds where IP, Ethernet, bandwidth, firewalls gets shared are prone to cross tenant attacks which can be mitigated using secured tunnels between the tenants. In VM hopping adversaries gain access to the physical hardware resources and is a critical issue in IaaS and PaaS clouds. Denial of service(DOS) attack is one more issue in multitenant shared cloud model where illegal users provoke denial of service by flooding the network port with undesirable packets. Man in the middle cryptographic attack is yet another risky problem where untrusted user positions between two trusted users of the cloud and intrude to access the data. Wrapping Attack is an MITM attack related to XML Signature wrapping attack where cloud users access cloud by means of the web services using duplications of login credentials. Browser attack induces data stealing through damaging the signature and encryption while translating the SOAP (Simple Object Access Protocol) messages between the web browser and web server.

- **Security challenges caused due to a shared kernel:** Virtualization empowers resource sharing by means of emulation of resources. The hypervisor-based virtualization offers sufficient isolation between guest virtual machines but then incurs significant overheads. In hypervisor-based virtualization several guest containers ride on top of host operating. Contrast to this, in container-based virtualization, the host operating system is virtualized so system without installing the additional kernel for the guest containers, which noticeably decreases the performance overhead. Container technology does not depend on a hypervisor to generate contained environment but hinge on kernel features like chroot, cgroups and namespaces. The multiple processes added to cgroups shares all the resources assigned to that group.

Even though namespaces and Linux kernel feature benefits container based virtualization, there occurs various security issues due to a shared kernel and weak isolation. Containers suffer from weak isolation owing to sharing of the system kernel. Any malicious code can affect other containers and underlying operating system. Such containers compromise the security of rest of the containers of the host machine and system as a whole. A user with root privileges on the container can mount and access any directory from the host even the root directory. This endangers the host to a threat called root breakout. A process that breaks out of the guest container gets equal access privileges on the host including root privileges. Host break in attack occurs on the allocated container when the host root gains access to containers and alters it. A user with uid =0 will be root on the host with complete root access rights even on the host. This causes threats like privilege escalation in which a user gets special rights like root users. The multi-tenant container cloud-based systems where multiple containers share the host resources are susceptible to threats like information leakage. Adversaries can take gain of these information leakage channels and initiate attack that upsets the confidentiality and integrity of the system.

The container daemon is unrestrained, which makes the applications in the container prone to security attacks through web interfaces. Malicious applications in the container tire out the system resources to a level. that other applications are inept to use them, for example, Denial Of service (DOS). The extra layer of isolation lacked by container makes it easy for attackers to launch into the host machine. Cloud container based environments with dearth of strong access control policies are disposed to cross site scripting attacks where the attacker implant client side script to the webpages.

The following security requirements are identified to be incorporated in CRC towards fostering the sharing of sensitive research resources:

Confidentiality of the data and applications: In collaborative environments where sensitive data and tools are shared among multiple researchers, it is imperative to apply methods to ensure that data and tools are not access by unauthorised users and are protected from malicious attacks. Shared resources get dispersed to many others without the awareness of the owner. Breach of confidentially could make researchers apprehensive in sharing data and applications with others. Hence techniques should be applied to guarantee that data and tools are not accessed by unauthorised users and are secured from malicious attacks.

Policy based access control: To address the owner's access control problem, there should be a mechanism to ensure that RO has complete control on his resources and must be able to stipulate who can use the resources and how. Research owner should be able to define the policy regarding user's permission on access the data and applications and the permitted activities on the resources. A researcher may request resources belonging to different research owners which necessitate a flexible mechanism that enables collaborative access control.

Monitoring and control: RO should be able to monitor the operations on the resources and get alerted if any anomaly occurs. Researcher's activities on the allocated resources need to monitored and any un authorised activity on the allocated data and application will be alerted.

6.3 Proposed Methodology

Based on the in depth review of the security concerns in cloud system, issues in container technology, collaborative research environments and existing mechanisms to mitigate the security issues, a security model for improving the isolation and security of container-based cloud systems is designed and integrated to access control model of CRC discussed in Section 4.5.

The proposed methodology consists the designing an enhanced access control model augmented with controlled object flow in CRC. The novel solution guarantees secured and controlled sharing of resources between researchers in collaborative research environment using a combination of secured containerisation, IFC-endorsed flow control and policy based access control.

The proposed approach ensures the confidentiality of the shared data and tools through containerisation and the containers are further secured by applying Linux security modules. Many existing approaches have used IFC to control and monitor data flow and control its propagation and the proposed approach have extended this capability to control the containers that enclose data sets, applications /tools and system environment.

The proposed approach prevails over dearth of scalability offered by ACL and rigid, role specific access control approach employed by RBAC by implementing a flexible policy based access control model. To accomplish an access control approach that is fine grained, Policy Enforcement Points (PEP) and related Policy Decision Points (PDP) are used that enforcing and defining the policies required for authorisation decisions. The policy based access control provide fine-grained authorisation mechanism that enable Research Owners (RO) to assign access privileges based on the policy enforced. The flexibility of the access control model empowers Research Owner to set access policy rights based on the roles and requirements of the different researchers.

6.4 Architectural Overview of the Enhanced Authorisation Model

The proposed access control mechanism facilitates the researchers to share resources bundled in secured containers, control and monitor the propagation of data and tools and specify an access control policy for the objects shared in collaborative research cloud. The unique features of the proposed approach are: Enhanced container isolation and security by implementing Linux security modules (LSM), IFC – endorsed flow control and monitoring and flexible policy based access control defined in XACML. Figure 6.1 illustrates an overview of enhanced access control model.

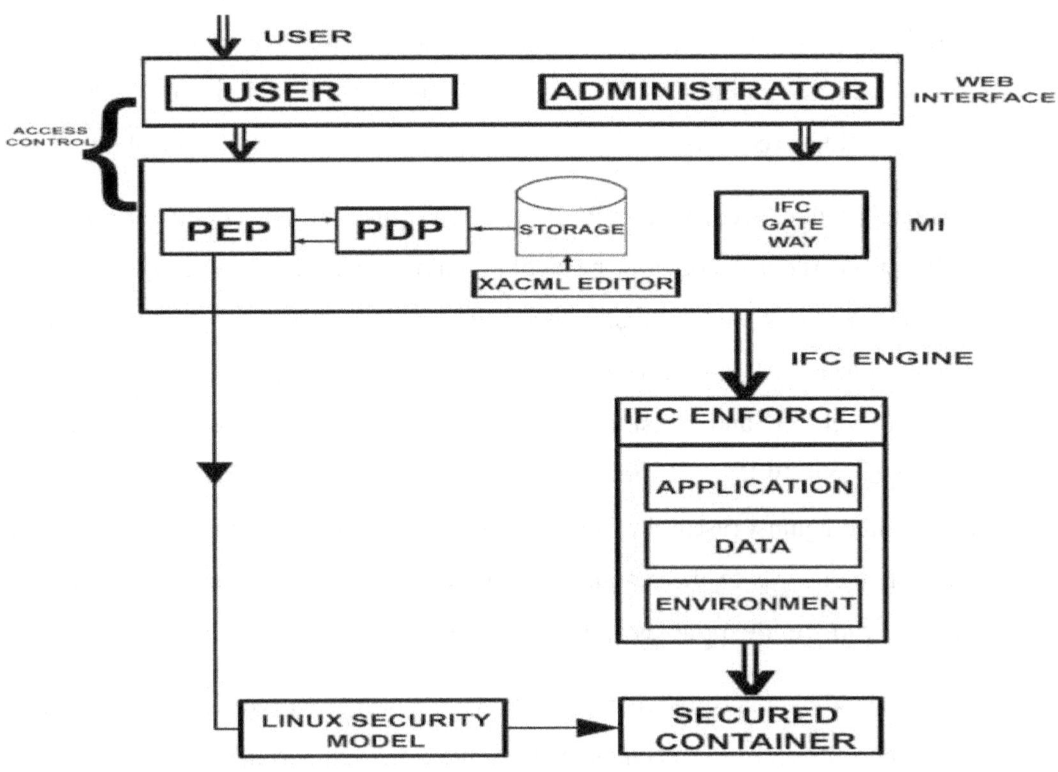

Figure 6. 1: Enhanced Access Control Model

The functionality of components of the proposed authorisation model in the following section.

Web interface: The web interface allows Researchers, Research Owners and Administrator to login and AAS authenticates the user in the research cloud. R_n request the resources through web interface. RO employs Management Interface (MI) to control the access to allocated resources and monitor it. MI also monitors the user activities on the allocated container objects and alerts the RO about any unauthorised activity. Administrator creates Apparmor profile by means of MI.

XACML editor: In CRC, PEP (Policy Enforcement Point) is firmly coupled with AAS. PEP receive the user request and forward to PDP. PDP evaluate the requests against the user policies and return a response to PEP. According to the response reviewed from PDP, PEP enforce the access control for the user. The XACML editor enables the administrator, in concurrence with RO to edit the XACML policies and uploaded to PDP.

Policy-based access control: The scalability and flexibility of the access control model is enhanced as we choose XACML as our policy language. XML based XACML let the administrators to enumerate and impose policies for authorisation. XACML adopts requests/response pattern to implement access control decisions.

The user policies are loaded in PDP. PEP forwards the user request for resources to PDP. Every request contains particulars of the user who request for resources (subject), process on the resource(action), resource (data, application, service, system component) and attributes. The policies loaded in Policy Decision Point (PDP) are verified, and decision whether user can access the resources or not, is send as a response to PEP which enforces the decision. Researchers' request for resources is evaluated against researcher's access control policy defined in PDP to determine whether the access to the resource can be allowed. Administrator in concurrence with RO can edit the policies and update the PDP.

The dynamic research requirements in a collaborative research environment necessitate a flexible mechanism that enables collaborative access control and support to multi-policy. The PEP is tightly coupled to AAS to enable credential verification. RO defines the access control rights on the container object (RCU objects) for any researcher. Administrator edits the XACML policy to set the access control privileges and upload the same to PDP. The flexible access control mechanism lets the RO modifies the privileges based on the needs of the researcher and the access privileges on the RCU.

Secured containerisation: Upon request from any researcher belonging to CRC, RO packages data and applications in the RCU. LXC technology provide portability and isolation for data, application by wrapping it in containers to enable the sharing of data and application among different researchers or collaborative groups. The pre-eminence of container isolation is that any process inside a container cannot impact a process in a different container. The container technology enables building images from the script, which gives an added advantage in terms of security as viewing the script before building the image would provide the means to detect any threats.

Even though container technology offers benefits like increased resource allocation efficiency, minimal performance overhead, the extent of isolation it provides to shared data and application is not strong enough to protect from security vulnerabilities. In CRC, R_n is granted root access privileges for that container using chroot, so that R_n can recreate the complete compute environment required to run the tools on the datasets. However, a user with root access privileges on the container may carry out actions like copy, print or recreate the applications in the container which will upset the confidentiality of data and applications. Any user with root privileges on the container can mount and access any directory from the host even the root directory. This exposes the host to a threat called root breakout [82] were root user in guest container can breakout and turnout to be root user of host.

In the CRC only RO and authorised users to whom the container is allocated have access rights on it. Even the host root does not have privilege to access to allocated container. Host break in [82] attack happens on the allocated container when the host root gain access to allocated containers and modifies it. A researcher with root user privileges also may list all the process running in the host, which is a threat to the security of the host.

In the proposed approach Apparmor provides security and isolation to the container, based on the Apparmor profile. Each authorised user in CRC have to mandatorily follow the access policies and privileges set in his Apparmor profile. Apparmor profile specifies accessible file path and capability entries specify execution rights on the RCU resources set for a particular researcher.

Hence allocated RCUs are protected from security vulnerabilities like attacks, host break in or root break out that may compromise the shared data and tools. Even with uid=0 for any user, access to the files not specified in Apparmor policy is not permitted and an occurrence of root break out is prevented. Apparmor does not permit host root with uid=0 to break in and access a resource inside the RCU. An Apparmor secured container can be accessed only by the authorised user and if any violation occurs it will be reported to MI.

Monitoring using MI: Researcher's operations on the allocated RCU is based on policy defined. MI verifies the defined policy and informs the RO if any unauthorised access has occurred. MI maintains a log of activities of users and resources. MI continuously monitors Apparmor log to ensure only authorised users can share the resources and any anomalies that occur in the RCU will be alerted. In enforcement mode any unauthorised activity by user MI will prevent such operations and prohibit the RCU from further operations. In compliance mode MI tracks the log, which can be reviewed any time.

IFC Gateway: IFC Gateway holds the label repository of researcher owners, researchers and RCU objects in the CRC .RO sets the secrecy and integrity labels for researcher who request for resources and allocated objects through IFC gateway. IFC engine creates the RCUs with IFC enforced objects.

IFC endorsed flow control: Discretionary Access Control (DAC) mechanisms namely Access Control List (ACL) and Role-Based Access Control (RBAC) ensures protection by regulating the access to the resources using access control checks within the applications. In Mandatory Access Control (MAC) approach, policies to ensure security of information is defined for the complete system. IFC (Information Flow Control) is a technique based on a MAC that expedite the tracking and securing of the data propagation .IFC realizes controlled and safe information flow by attaching labels with data and with principals who wish to access the data.

IFC enforces a strategy that guarantees confidentiality and integrity for the data and applications that are shared between researchers using secrecy labels ("no read up, no write down") [31] and integrity label ("no read down, no write up") [84].

Many existing approaches have used IFC labels for controlled exchange of data or information. The proposed solution extended this ability to enable RO to restrain the objects he shares with other researchers .RO set the access rights on the container objects. RO applies IFC labels on his container objects and specifies the security constraints on them according to each researcher defined policy already set by administrator. RO has complete ownership of his resources and only solely privileged to set the IFC labels and modify the security constraints. The administrator even with root access privileges does not have ownership rights for RO's data and application. MI alerts RO regarding any unauthorised activities on the shared resources.

6.4.1 Security Module

The schematic diagram of proposed security model id as shown in Figure 6.2. A defined user policy is set for every authenticated user who logins to the system. Security model maps the file path of each container object against a user and each PID is consecutively mapped against user security table. The security table retains an index of all file paths and PID. It similarly maintains a log of all the container operations going on in the system.

The two-way authorization mechanism validates object file path against the user policy and therefore checks that only authorized users who have a valid file path entry in security table accesses the container. Even the host root is not permitted to access the container because it does not have a file path entry in security table. Each PID is mapped to the user so that any user without a mapping to PID will be denied the access to the container objects.

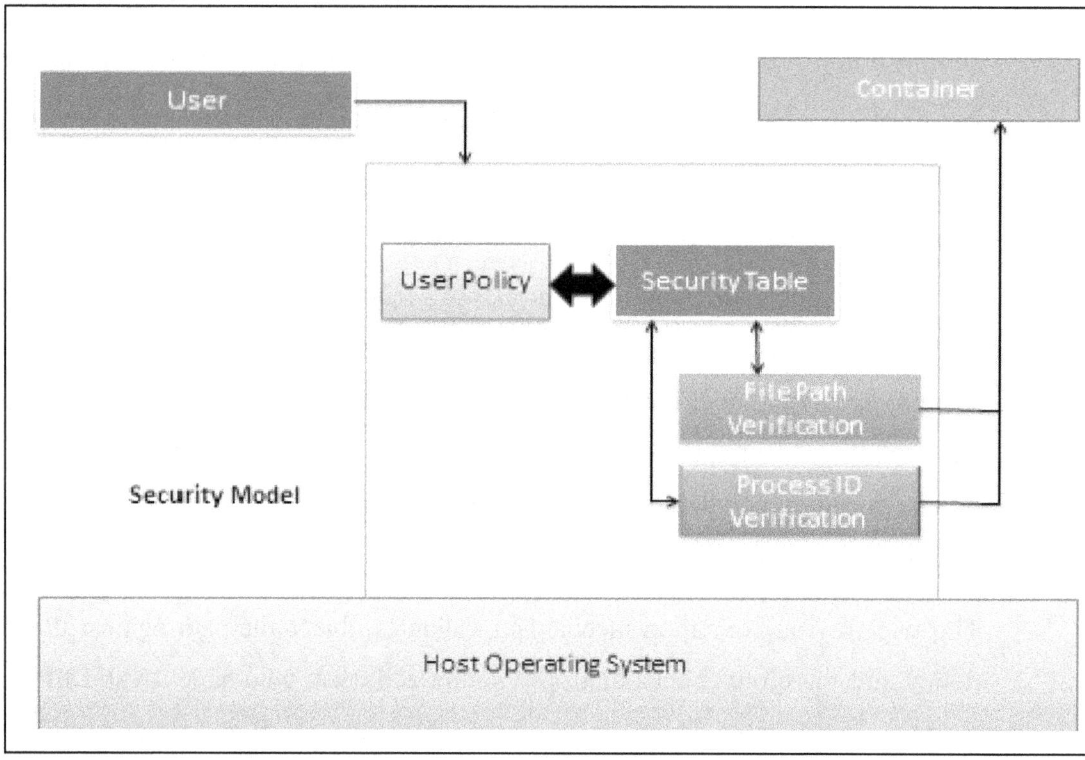

Figure 6. 2: Schematic Diagram of Security Module

6.4.2 IFC Enabled Isolation for Inter container and Intra container Sharing

IFC allows fine grained non-interference policy, ensuring confidentiality and isolation for inter container and intra container data and tool sharing. RCUs may contain many applications and different datasets .RO can secure the datasets and control the flow such that only to application which has relevant security labels can access it. RO specifies which application can access which data set in IFC gateway and user's Apparmor profile .RO sets secrecy labels for each RCU objects and user. Accessible file path and privileges of objects and user are set in Apparmor profile. User may request for different data sets and applications which may necessitate setting secrecy labels access container boundaries.

Figure 6.3 illustrates inter container isolation where RO allocates R_1 application A and B with data sets C and D in container 1. RO can set a policy that application A can access only data set C and can isolate data set D from application A and application B can access C and D.

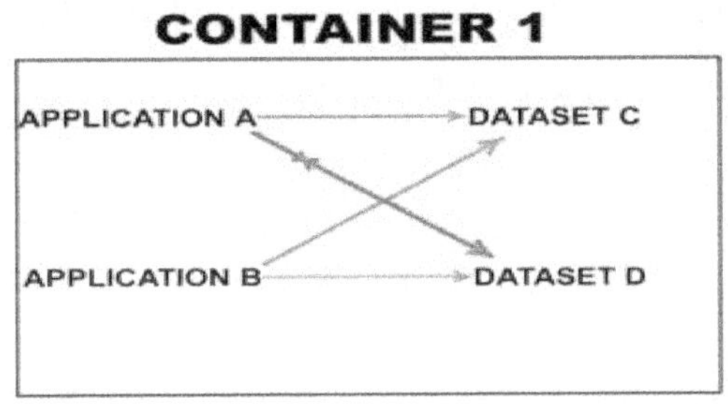

Figure 6. 3: Inter Container Isolation

IFC enabled Intra container isolation is demonstrated in Figure 6.4. RO has allocated Container 1 and Container 2 for same user R_1 with application A and data sets C and D. IFC ensures isolation between the two containers such that application A in container 1 cannot access datasets in other container, unless specified in the policy.

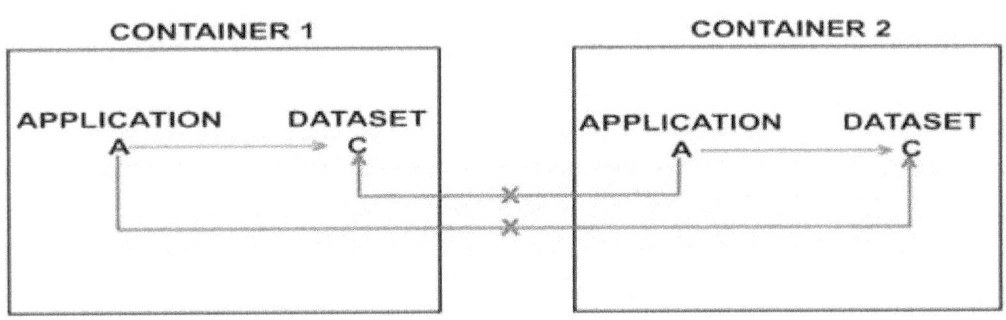

Figure 6. 4: Intra Container Isolation

. Even though R_n is granted full access rights on the allocated container objects, IFC enables RO to have complete control on his data and applications. Hence, .IFC persistently enforces the defined policies even when the resources have been shared.

6.5 Mathematical Modelling

Each object in CRC is attached with secrecy label and integrity label.

$S(R_n)$ = secrecy label of a researcher R_n, S(RO) = secrecy label of RO

$I(R_n)$ = integrity label of researcher R_n, I(RO) = integrity label of RO

RO will share requested data or application with any other researcher when secrecy labels matches and R_n will accept the resources only if integrity labels matches.

Any RO in CRC will share data or application with researcher R_n only if,

$RO \rightarrow R_n$, iff $S(R_n) \subseteq S(RO) \wedge I(R_n) \subseteq I(RO)$ (1)

RO may have to change the access permissions on the RCU objects after allocation is done also. This can be achieved by adding or removing privileges in the secrecy label and the integrity label. Thus the security levels can be altered through variation in secrecy labels. Alteration in the integrity labels reflects variation in authencity of the shared resources.

P_s^+ denotes privilege of RO to add or remove secrecy label for R_n

P_x^+ denotes privilege of RO to add or remove secrecy label or integrity label for R_n

RO has privilege to the alter the security conditions set for R_n by adding or removing a tag 't'.

Adding secrecy label is denoted as $t \in P_s^{++}(RO)$ and remove a secrecy label denoted as

$t \in P_s^-(RO)$ and likewise for integrity label.

A variation of a label RO ~ RO 'is safe when,

$X(RO') = X(RO) \cup \{t\}$ if $t\in t \in P_x^+(RO)$ (2)

or

$X(RO') = X(RO) \cup \{t\}$ if $t\in t \in P_x^-(RO)$ (3)

For example, an R_n without privilege labels cannot copy or share the data or application.

6.6 Algorithmic implementation

The proposed solution for secured object flow control permits safe and confidential sharing of resources. Upon login the researchers 's credentials set in

PVC R_n (AAS) is verified by AAS. PEP enforces user policy R_n (UP) defined in PDP. User credentials is a combination credentials set in AAS and user policy enforced by PEP. This supplements the security of user id and password based authentication. In proposed approach user policy defined in PDP using XACML is also verified by MI. Secrecy labels $S(R_n)$, S(RO) and integrity labels $I(R_n)$, I(RO)are applied to RO and R_n and the RCU objects as well. Resource sharing is enabled only if these labels are matching. Apparmor profile $R_n(A)$ is function of file path of an object, privilege set for that object.

A random variable SF is a function of secrecy labels, integrity labels of RO and R_n. This function is defined to enhance flexibility in secured object flow. If SF=1 when secrecy label of RO matches with R_n and likewise for integrity labels and SF=0 means that either of the labels does not match with each other and the sharing of resources is not permitted. Therefore, this novel approach enables to achieve flexibility in secured object flow control.

Algorithm 1: Algorithm for secured object flow control.

Assumptions:

R_n : researcher

R_n (AAS): user credentials set in PVC of the researcher.

R_n (UP): user policy in PDP

$R_n(P)$: authenticated user policy

$R_n(A)$: user's Apparmor profile

$S(R_n)$: secrecy label of a Rn

S(RO): secrecy label of RO

$I(R_n)$: integrity label of R_n

I(RO): integrity label of RO

X : file path of a container object set in Apparmor profie

Y: privilege of an object in specified file path

SF : random variable.

Step 1: User credentials R_n (AAS) verified in AAS server and R_n log in to CRC.

Step 2: R_n request resources (data/application/results)

Step 3: PEP verifies user's request for resources.

Step 4: PEP sends user request in to PDP.

Step 5: PDP verifies the stored user policy, R_n (UP).

Step 6: If user request accords with user policy, PEP enforces user policy $R_n(P)$

$R_n(P) = R_n (AAS) + R_n (UP)$ go to step 10

Step 7: else user request is denied and it is send to MI.

Step 8: MI verifies the request from RO.

Step 9: MI update the user policy through XACML policy editor and update the PDP Go to step 5.

Step 10: user's request for resources send to RO

Step 11: RO applies the IFC labels $S(R_n)$ S(RO), $I(R_n)$, I(RO) to objects And creates RCU

Step 12: if $f(S(R_n), S(RO)) \wedge f(I(R_n), I(RO)$

SF =1

else

SF=0

Step 13: update the label repository.

Step 14: RO approves the privileges for user and objects.

Step 15: Apparmor profile $R_n(A) = f(X, Y)$ created for each user.

Step 16: authenticated user to access the allocated RCU if only if the Apparmor profile exist.

if X, Y=1

$R_n(A) = 1$

else

$R_n(A) = 0$

Step 17: MI verifies user policy, IFC labels, user's Apparmor profile.

Step 18: If $R_n(P) \wedge (R_n(A) \wedge SF) = 1$ then

R_n get access and execution rights on the RCU

6.7 Performance Isolation Benchmarking

Although containerization derives plenty of benefits like improved resource allocation efficacy and negligible performance overheads, the expanse of isolation is not robust enough to defend from security susceptibilities. Increased isolation increases the security and offers protection from security concerns. The performance isolation of the CRC framework was evaluated by carrying out stress tests, with Open source, Linux based benchmarking tool **httperf.** The stress tests performed are Network test, CPU intensive test and Fork bomb test. httperf is generally used to benchmarking web server performance by creating server workloads. Benchmarking the webserver performance facilitates the variation of number of users with varying workloads. This can be easily done by using httperf as the benchmarking marking tool in this experiment.

CPU intensive test was done using the tool Stress-ng by creating multiple workloads to stress CPU using floating point calculations. Network stress test was performed using **iperf 3**, by creating 6 instances of 60 KB over UDP and transmitted. Fork bomb test generates the denial of service (DOS) and consumes the resources by looping that produces new child processes. Fork bomb works on CPU cycles and saturates the system.

6.7.1 Experimental Setup

Six machines with Core i7 -8565U processors, 4.6 GHz ,128 GB RAM and 4- core are connected through 24 port Layer 2 CISCO switch. RCU systems were constituted by installing Openstack on Ubuntu 14.04 with and four LXD containers. Three containers were created one running httperf and two running Apache webserver 8.5, connected via Ethernet at 10GBps.One webserver was configured in LXD and other in RCU. The test suite included stress tests for CPU, Network transmit and receive and a fork bomb, that were performed on RCU and native LXD. The performance isolation of CRC augmented with secured container based access control model was evaluated. A webserver was configured in RCU and algorithm for secured object flow control is implemented using python. Stress tests and fork bomb test were conducted on RCU and secured RCU and benchmarking was performed.

6.7.2 Result Analysis

The results of stress tests and fork bomb tests conducted on the LXD and RCU is as shown in Table 6.1. The results of stress tests and fork bomb tests conducted on the RCU and secured RCU is as shown in Table 6.2

Reply time is very crucial in web server performance. As shown in Table 6.1 the CPU stress test with 3400 Connection request the reply time for LXD is 1400 ms where as in RCU it is 1.8 ms. This shows there is no performance degradation in

RCU. The results show that with fork bomb test the reply time of LXD is 380 ms and RCU responds with in .74 ms. This clearly indicates RCU is well isolated and child process creation by fork bombing does not impact RCU. The results for Network test indicates the reply time of LXD is 1400 ms and for RCU it is 1.4 ms

Table 6. 1: Results of stress tests on RCU and LXD using httperf

CPU Intensive test	**LXD**	**RCU**
Connection request (3400)/replies	3200	3400
Connection rate (conn/sec)	268	278
Reply time (ms)	1400	1.8
Net I/O (KB/sec)	92	104
Test - duration (sec)	12.7	12.3
Fork bomb test		
Connection request (638) /replies	174	174
Connection rate(conn/sec)	132	164
Reply time (ms)	380	0.74
Net I/O (KB/sec)	24	32
Test - duration (sec)	26.7	19.13
Network test		
Connection request (3400)/replies	3400	3400
Connection rate (conn/sec)	262	278
Reply time (ms)	1400	1.4
Net I/O (KB/sec)	92	104
Test -duration (sec)	12.9	12.2

Table 6. 2: Results of stress tests on RCU and secured RCU using httperf

CPU Test	**RCU**	**RCU with LSM +IFC**
Connection request (3400)/replies	3400	3400
Connection rate (conn/sec)	278	394
Reply time (sec)	1.8	0.91
Net I/O (KB/sec)	104	179
Test -duration (sec)	12.3	10.6

Fork bomb test		
Connection request (638)/replies	174	324
Connection rate(conn/sec)	164	210
Reply time (sec)	0.74	0.32
Net I/O (KB/sec)	32	101
Test- duration (sec)	19.13	14.12
Network test		
Connection request (3400)/replies	3400	3400
Connection rate(conn/sec)	278	394
Reply time (sec)	1.4	0.91
Net I/O (KB/sec)	104	179
Test - duration (sec)	12.2	10.6

6.7.3 Comparitive Analysis

In CPU, network test there is minimal change in connection rate, connection replies, test duration, Net I/O with RCU. But the reply time reduces substantially from 1.4 sec to 1.8 ms that point to a very trustworthy and steady connection with improved response and enhanced throughput. In Fork bomb test, RCU exhibited a considerable improvement in connection rate (132 to 164), Net I/O (24 KB/sec to 32 KB/sec), test duration (19.13 sec to 26.7 Sec) and reply time (380 ms to 0.74 ms). Figure 6. 5 demonstrates the performance isolation benchmarking of RCU. Thus RCU is better isolated from interferences and secured from security attacks.

During CPU stress test, the reply time for secured RCU is 0.91 ms. Hence the secured RCU has better performance due to proposed algorithm. In fork bomb test the reply time of RCU is 0.32 ms. Figure 6. 6 shows the performance isolation benchmarking of secured RCU. Hence it is evident that the CRC framework is secured and protected from security vulnerabilities.

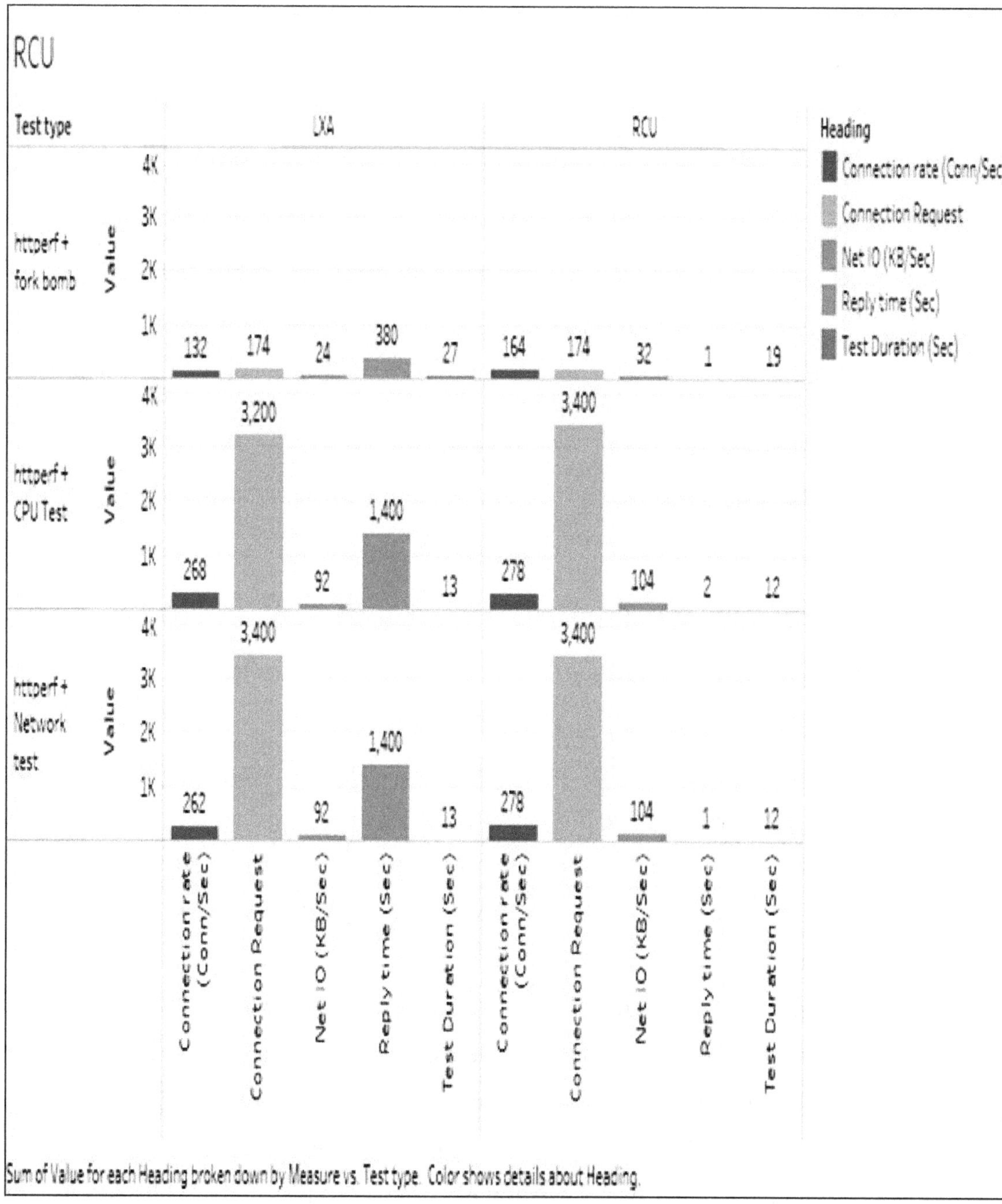

Figure 6. 5: Performance Isolation Benchmarking of RCU

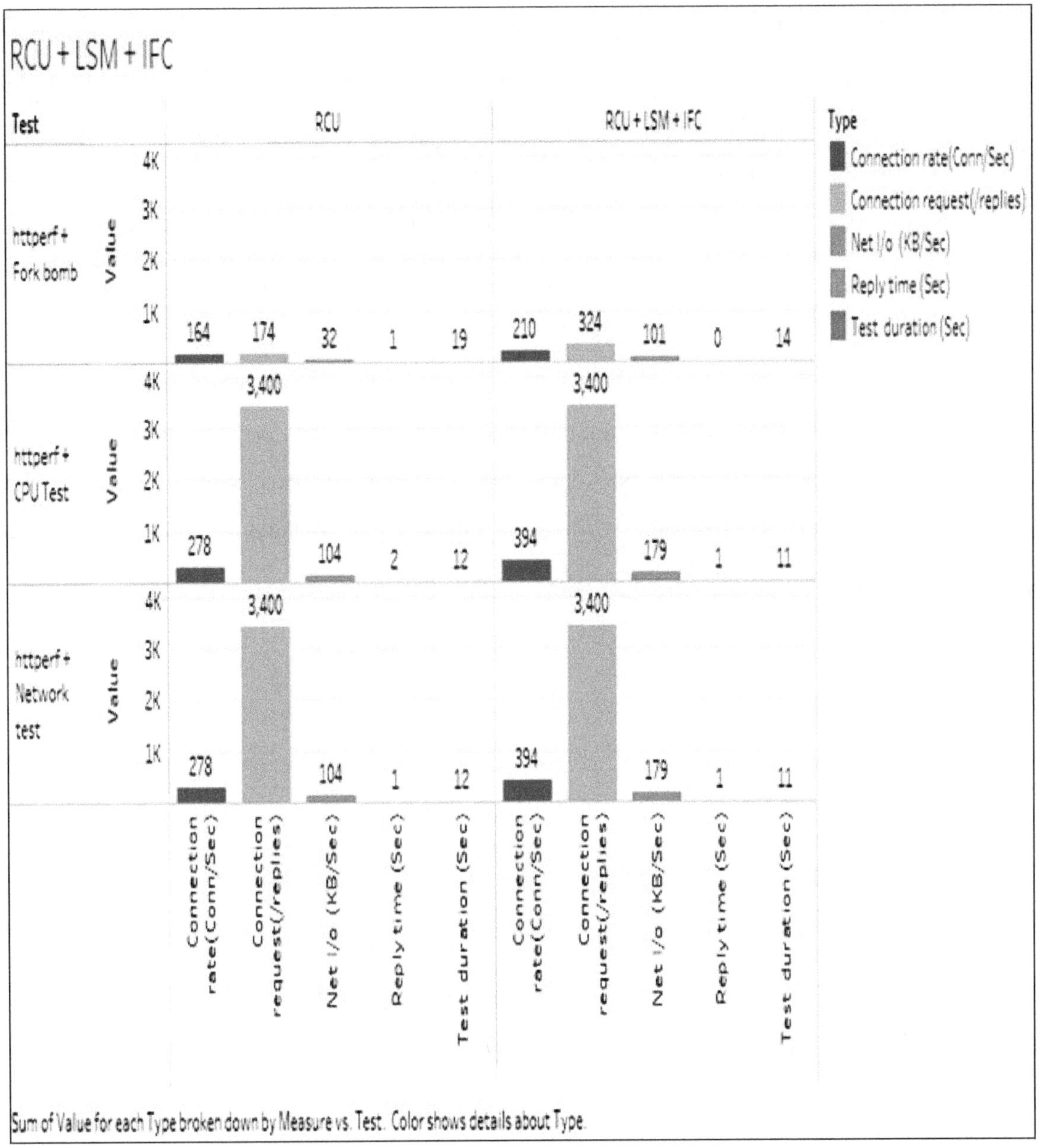

Figure 6. 6: Performance Isolation Benchmarking of Secured RCU

6.8 Summary

The chapter has discussed the security challenges in cloud based environments, container virtualization, concerns in sharing data, tools and results in collaborative research. The proposed for algorithm a secured object flow control offers much more than traditional security to meet up the dynamic, ad-hoc nature of research clouds.

performance isolation benchmarking of RCU. The performance isolation benchmarking demonstrates that RCU is well isolated from interferences and secured from security attacks. The proposed model augments the isolation and security of the cloud container-based environment and supports the secure sharing of the sensitive research data and applications across such public hosted collaboration platforms with a strong access control approach that assures confidentiality and authorized access.

CHAPTER 7

CHAPTER-7

CONCLUSIONS AND FUTURE SCOPE

7.1 Preface

This chapter summarizes the research work titled cloud container framework with hybrid access control and security for collaborative research. The chapter elaborates the contributions of the research, discusses the scope, limitations and future work.

7.2 Conclusion

This thesis has suggested and examined a suite of unique methods towards the design of collaborative research framework grounded on cloud that serves a complete compute environment for researchers. The proposed research work has attempted to resolve the challenges identified in prevailing cloud-based frameworks for research collaboration. The theoretical background of the proposed study, formulated research problems, inspiration, purpose and methodology for this research work is enumerated in Chapter 1. A comprehensive review about existent collaborative research frameworks, virtualization, resource provisioning methods security apprehensions in cloud and dominant security mechanisms are presented in Chapter 2. This near-exhaustive review helped to identify the research gaps and articulate the research questions. Chapter 3 details the design requirements and high level architecture of proposed Collaborative Research Cloud framework. Along with this, the research methodology used in the approach is also explained. Chapter 4 describes the authentication and authorisation in the proposed framework. Additionally, this chapter has presented proposed algorithms for user creation and login process and evaluation of performance efficiency in terms of creation time and finish time. The novel techniques and algorithms are proposed in Chapter 5 addresses the problems in dynamic resource provisioning due to fluctuating resource demands in collaborative research set-ups. Extensive result analysis and comparative analysis with existing systems are also presented in the chapter. Chapter 6 has discussed security concerns in cloud systems and need to enhance the cloud security to facilitate secured sharing of sensitive research resources in research cloud platforms. The proposed access control model and algorithms have proved to improve the confidentiality and privacy of shared resources. The implementation of system prototype of CRC framework in Open stack and further evaluation of the performance and isolation, with detailed analysis of results and benchmarking is well explained in Chapter 6.

7.3 Research Contribution

The thesis has identified some of the major concerns in cloud based collaborative research frameworks and has attempted to design unique solutions to address the problems. The key contributions of the research are:

- The thesis has introduced the deployment of cloud container technology for sharing data, application and resources in collaborative research frameworks, which is a very unique and exceptional approach. The robustness of proposed endorses the selection of resources as per the research requirements and researcher owners can define access privileges on his resources. The thesis has presented the novel approach of flexible, portable customized containers to spawn complete computational environment.
- The thesis has presented the design of flexible, fine grained access control model to ensure security and confidentiality in cloud based collaborative research environment: The role based access control models deployed in collaborative research clouds are inadequate to provide the flexibility to the owner, to define the access control policy for his resources that are shared. The collaborating researchers must able to define the access control policy and monitor and control the propagation of shared resources. which necessitate a flexible mechanism that enables collaborative access control. The unique features of the proposed access control model are enhanced container isolation and security by implementing Linux security modules (LSM), IFC endorsed flow control, monitoring and flexible policy based access control defined in XACML. Thus the proposed framework ensures flexibility and also addresses access control problem.
- Novel algorithms are proposed and implemented to accomplish
    - dynamic resource provisioning and optimization of the resource utilization.

- Secured object flow control.

The prevailing collaborative research platforms, domain specific e-infrastructures and science clouds delivers functionalities like data storage, document archiving, data harvesting, retrieval or resource allocation. None of them has offered a complete platform that facilitates secured sharing of data and tools, reproducibility of compute environments, dynamic resource provisioning and user defined policies for access control. Therefore, the proposed research work has attempted to make a make a very significant contribution in area of collaborative research.

7.4 Limitations.

The limitations of the proposed study are as following:

- The proposed research study is limited only to scientific collaborative research.
- Cost efficiency evaluation of the framework is not investigated in this research work.

7.5 Future Scope of Work

The potentials of future scope of work that evolved from this research work is as follows:

- Future development in this domain of research can be directed towards developing a parallel processing algorithm for optimal residual resource allocation in a high performance computing and symmetric multiprocessing environments.
- New technology trends like software defined computing and server less computing can be incorporated to the collaborative research framework to add further elasticity and robustness.

REFERENCES

REFERENCES

[1] AbdulrahmanAzab, DianaDomanska,"Software Provisioning Inside a Secur e Environment as Docker Containers Using Stroll File-System" 2016 16th IEEE/ACM International Symposium on Cluster, Cloud and Grid Computing (Grid), pp: 674 – 683, 2016.

[2] Adam Brinckman, Donald Luc, Jarek Nabrzyski, Gary L. Neidig, Joel Neidig, Tyler A. Puckett, Swapna Krishnakumar Radha, Ian J. Taylor, "A Comparative Evaluation of Blockchain Systems for Application Sharing Using Containers", 2017 IEEE 13th International Conference on e-Science (e-Science), pp: 490 – 499, 2017.

[3] Alexander Ngenzi, Selvarani R, Suchithra "FDMC: Framework for Decision Making in Cloud for Efficient Resource Management", International Journal of Electrical and Computer Engineering (IJECE), Vol. 7, No. 1, pp: 496~504 ISSN: 2088-8708, DOI: 10.11591/ijece. v7i1.pp496-504,2017

[4] Antcheva I, Ballintijn M, Bellenot B, Biskup M, Brun R, Buncic N, Canal Ph., Casadei D, Couet O, Fine V, Franco L, GanisG, Gheata A, Maline D Gonzalez, Goto M, Iwaszkiewicz J, Kreshuk A, Segura D Marcos, Maunder R, Moneta L, Naumann A, Offermann E, Onuchin V, Panacek S, Rademakers F, Russo P, Tadel M. ROOT – A C++ framework for petabyte data storage, statistical analysis and visualization. Computer Physics Communications. 2009;180(12):2499–2512.

[5] Arnon Rosenthal, PeterMork, Maya HaoLi, Jean Stanford, David Koester, Patti Reynolds, "Cloud computing: A new business paradigm for biomedical information sharing", Journal of Biomedical Informatics Vol.43, Issue 2, pp:342–353, 2010.

[6] Asgari, Bahar & Ghobaei-Arani, Mostafa & Jabbehdari, Sam, "An Effiecient Approach for Resource Auto-Scaling in Cloud Environments", International Journal of Electrical and Computer Engineering (IJECE), Vol.6, No.5, pp: 2415-2424, 2016.

[7] B. Balamurugan, S. Linkesh, E. Durga Chowdary, "Unified RB-DAC Approach with Secure Authentication Using Smart Card Architecture", Eco-Friendly Computing and Communication Systems (ICECCS), IEEE, pp: 161-165, 2014.

[8] Bastian Roth, Robin Hecht, Bernhard Volz, Stefan Jablonskil., "Towards a Generic Cloud-based Virtual Research Environment", Computer Software and Applications Conference Workshops (COMPSACW), pp.267 – 272, 2011.

[9] BrunoYujiLino,Kimura,"Workload regressionbased resource provisioning f or small cloud providers", In Proceedings of IEEE Symposium on Computers and Communication (ISCC), pp: 295 – 301, 2016.

[10] C. Myers and B. Liskov, "A decentralized model for information flow control," in Proc. 17th Symp. Oper. Syst. Principles, pp:129–142, 1997.

[11] Carl Boettiger, "An introduction to Docker for reproducible research, with examples from the R environment", ACM SIGOPS Operating Systems Review - Special Issue on Repeatability and Sharing of Experimental Artifacts", Vol.49, Issue 1, pp:71-79, 2015.

[12] Charles Ferreira Gonçalves," Benchmarking the Security of Virtualization Infrastructures: Motivation and Approach", IEEE International Symposium on Software Reliability Engineering Workshops (ISSREW), pp. 100 – 103, 2017.

[13] D. Bender," Privacy and security issues in cloud computing," in Proc, Comput. Internet Lawyer, pp. 1_15, 2012.

[14] D. E. Bell and L. J. LaPadula, "Secure Computer Systems: Mathematical Foundations and Model", The MITRE Corp., Bedford MA, Tech. Rep. M74-244, 1973.

[15] D. E. Denning, "A lattice model of secure information flow", Commun. ACM, vol. 19, no. 5, pp: 236–243, 1976.

[16] D. Ferraiolo, R. Kuhn, "Role-Based Access Controls", In:15th NISTNCSC National Computer Security Conference, Bultimore Maryland, USA, pp:554-563, 1992.

[17] Danan Thilakanathan, Shiping Chen, Surya Nepal, Rafael Calvo, "Safe Protect: Controlled Data Sharing with User-Defined Policies in Cloud

based Collaborative Environment" IEEE Transactions on Emerging Topics in Computing, Volume: 4, Issue: 2, Pages: 301 – 315, Year: 2016.

[18] Dan Gonzales, Jeremy M. Kaplan, Evan Saltzman, Zev Winkelman, Dulani Woods, "Cloud-Trust—a Security Assessment Model for Infrastructure as a Service (IaaS) Clouds", IEEE Transactions on Cloud Computing, Volume: 5, Issue: 3, pp: 523 – 536, 2017.

[19] Elaheh kheiri, Mostafa Ghobaei Arani, Reyhaneh Kheiri, Alireza Taghizadeh, "An Approach based on Genetic Algorithm or multi-tenant Resource Allocation in SaaS Applications", IAES International Journal of Artificial Intelligence (IJ-AI) Vol. 6, No. 3, pp: 124~138, 2017.

[20] Fernández Albor Víctor, Seco Marcos, Méndez Muñoz Víctor, Fernández Tomás, Silva Pena Juán Saborido, Graciani Diaz Ricardo.Multivariate," Analysis of Variance for High Energy Physics Software in Virtualized Environments", International Symposium on Grids and Clouds,160:1–15. 2015

[21] Gholami, Ali & Laure, Erwin, "Security and Privacy of Sensitive Data in Cloud Computing: A Survey of Recent Developments", Computer Science & Information Technology, 5. 10.5121/csit.2015.51611, 2016.

[22] Hassan Takabi, James B.D. Joshi, Gail-Joon Ahn," Security and Privacy Challenges in Cloud Computing Environments", IEEE Security & Privacy, Volume: 8, Issue: 6, pp: 24 – 31, 2010.

[23] Ibrahim Alobaidan, Michael Mackay, Posco Tso," Build trust in the cloud computing - Isolation in container based virtualization", 9th International Conference on Developments in eSystems Engineering, pp:143-148, 2016.

[24] Ibrahim K Musa1, StuartDWalker, AnneMOwen, Andrew P Harrison, "Self-service infrastructure container for data intensive application", Journal of Cloud Computing: Advances, Systems and Applications 2014, 3:5.

[25] J Sylvan Katz, Ben R. martin; Why research collaboration, Research policy 26(19917) 1-18

[26] Jean Bacon, David Eyers, Thomas F. J.-M. Pasquier, Jatinder Singh, Ioannis Papagiannis, Peter Pietzuch," Information Flow Control for Secure Cloud Computing", IEEE Transactions on Network and Service Management, Volume: 11, Issue:1, pp: 76 – 89, 2014.

[27] Jeeva Chelladhurai, Pethuru Raj Chelliah, Sathish Alampalayam Kumar, "Securing Docker Containers from Denial of Service (DoS) Attacks", IEEE International Conference on Services Computing (SCC), pp: 856 – 859, 2016.

[28] Jiajun Zhang, Xiaohui Liang, Zhikun Zhang, Shibo He, Zhiguo ShiRe-DPoctor, "Real-Time Health Data Releasing with W-Day DifferentialPrivacyGLOBECOM", IEEE Global Communications Conference, pp: 1 – 6, 2017.

[29] Joost B. Wagenaar, Benjamin H. Brinkmann, Zachary Ives, Gregory A. Worrell, and Brian Litt, Benjamin H. Brinkmann, "A Multimodal Platform for Cloud-based Collaborative Research "In Proceedings of IEEE EMBS Conference on Neural Engineering", pp. 1386 - 1389 ,2013.

[30] Jyoti Shetty, Sahana Upadhaya, Rajarajeshwari HS, Shobha G, Jayant Chandra, "An Empirical Performance Evaluation of Docker Con-tainer, Openstack Virtual Machine and Bare Metal Server ", Indonesian Journal of Electrical Engineering and Computer Science, Vol. 7, No. 1, pp. 205 ~ 213, July 2017.

[31] K. J. Biba, "Integrity Considerations for Secure Computer Systems," MITRE Corp., Tech. Rep. ESD-TR 76-372, 1977.

[32] K. Peffers, t. Tuunanen, m. A. Rothenberger, and s. Chatterjee, "A Design Science Research Methodology for Information Systems Research," Journal of Management Information Systems, vol. 24, no. 3, pp. 45–77, 2007.

[33] Kalyanam, Rajesh & Campbell, Rob & Kearney, Derrick & Delgass, Leif & Biehl, Larry & Zhao, Lan & Ellis, Carolyn & Song, Carol. (2017). Cloud-enabling a Collaborative Research Platform, "Cloud-enabling a Collaborative Research Platform: The GABBs Story", PEARC17 in Proceedings of the Practice and Experience in Advanced Research Computing, Article No: 23,2017.

[34] Kate Keahey and Tim Freeman, "Science clouds: Early experiences in cloud computing for scientific applications," in Proceedings of Cloud Computing and Application Workshop, pp: 825–830, 2008.

[35] Khaled El Emam, Fida Kamal Dankar, "Protecting Privacy Using k-AnonymityJ", Am Med Inform Assoc, 15(5): 627–637. doi: 10.1197/jamia.M2716], 2008.

[36] Klein, J. (1994). Finding interdisciplinary knowledge and information. In J. Klein & W. Doty (Eds.), Interdisciplinary Studies Today.

[37] Lopez-Garcia, Alvaro & Fernández, Enol & Orviz Fernandez, Pablo & Campos Plasencia, Isabel & Marco de Lucas, Jesús, "Resource provisioning in Science Clouds: Requirements and challenges", Software: Practice and Experience, 48. 10.1002/spe.2544, 2017.

[38] M A Rizvi, Anupriya Shrivastava,"External authentication approach for virtual private network using LDAP", First International Conference on Networks & Soft Computing (ICNSC2014), pp. 50 – 54, 2014.

[39] M. Dalton, C. Kozyrakis, and N. Zeldovich, "Nemesis: preventing authentication & access control vulnerabilities in web applications", USENIX Security Symposium, 2009.

[40] M. Thangapandiyan, P.M. Rubesh Anand, "A secure and reputation based recommendation framework for cloud services", IEEE International Conference on Computational Intelligence and Computing Research (ICCIC), pp: 1 – 4, 2016.

[41] Mardhani Riasetiawan; Ahmad Kamil Mahmood," Science-Forge: A collaborative scientific framework "IEEE Symposium on Industrial Electronics and Applications (ISIEA) pp: 665 – 668, 2010

[42] Marty Humphrey; Jacob Steele; In Kee Kim; Michael G. Kahn; Jessica Bondy; Michael Ames, "CloudDRN: A Lightweight, End-to end System for Sharing Distributed Research Data in the Cloud", In Proceedings of IEEE 9th International Conference on e-Science, PP. 254 – 26,2013.

[43] McGregor, A & Bennett, D & Majumdar, S & Nandy, Biswajit & Melendez, J.O. & St-Hilaire, M & Lau, D & Liu, J, "A Cloud-Based Platform for Supporting Research Collaboration", In Proceedings of IEEE 8th International Conference on Cloud Computing, pp: 1107 – 1110,2015.

[44] Miguel G. Xavi-er, Marcelo V. Neves, Fabio D. Rossi, Tiago C. Fer-reto, Timoteo Lange, Cesar A. F. De Rose, "Performance evaluation of container based virtualization for High Performance Computing Environments", Eu-romicro International Conference on Parallel, Distributed, and Network-Based Processing, IEEE, pp: 233 – 240, Year: 2013

[45] Ms. Disha H. Parekh, Dr. R. Sridaran, "An Analysis of Security Challenges in Cloud Computing", International Journal of Advanced Computer Science and Applications, Vol. 4, No.1, pp: 46, 2013.

[46] Muhamad Fitra Kacamarga, Bens Pardamean, Hari Wijaya, "Lightweight Virtualization in Cloud Computing for Research", Communications in Computer and Information Science VOL.516 Springer International Publishing., pp. 439–445, 2015.

[47] Naseer Amara, Huang Zhiqui, Awais Ali, "Cloud Computing Security Threats and Attacks with Their Mitigation Techniques", International Conference on Cyber-Enabled Distributed Computing and Knowledge Discovery (CyberC), pp: 244 – 251, 2017.

[48] Nitin Nagar, Pradeep k. Jatav, "International Journal of Advanced Computer Research (ISSN (print): 2249-7277 ISSN (online): 2277-7970)", A Secure Authenticate Framework for Cloud Computing Environment, Volume-4, Number-1, Issue-14, pp: 266, 2014.

[49] Sri Nagesh, Tapas Kumar, Vedula Venkateswara rao," A Survey on Security Aspects of Server Virtualization in Cloud Computing", International Journal of Electrical and Computer Engineering (IJECE) Vol. 7, No. 3, pp: 1326~1336, June 2017.

[50] Rachana Oza, Ritesh Patel, Ankita Desai," An Application of Hybrid ACL Approach in Cloud Environment", 2nd International Conference on Advances in Computer Science & Applications [CSA – 2013] Volume 5 Pages 583 – 590, 2013.

[51] Rahul wargad and manimala puri, "A study of cloud computing based model to facilitate collaborative research", IJAEDU- International E-Journal of Advances in Education, Vol. I, Issue 2, pp: 142-148, 2015.

[52] Raquel Almeida; Naaliel Mendes; Henrique Madeira," Sharing Experimental and Field Data: The AMBER Raw Data Repository Experience", IEEE 30th International Conference on Distributed Computing Systems Workshops, pp. 313 – 320, 2010.

[53] Russell A Poldrack& Krzysztof J Gorgolewski1, "Making big data open: data sharing in neuroimaging", VOLUME 17, NUMBER 11, Nature neuroscience, 2014,

[54] S Nepal, RO Sinnott, C Friedrich, C Wise, S Chen, S Kanwal, J Yao, "TruXy: Trusted storage cloud for scientific workflows", IEEE transactions on cloud computing, volume: 5, issue: 3, pp: 428 – 442, 2017.

[55] S. Shin, K. Kobara, and H. Imai, ``A secure public cloud storage sys-tem," in Proc. Int. Conf. Internet Technol. Secured Trans. (ICITST), pp. 103_109, 2011.

[56] Sandhu, R. S., & Samarati, P, "Access control: principle and practice". Communications Magazine, IEEE,32(9), pp: 40-48, 1994.

[57] Sherif T, Rioux P, Rousseau ME, Kassis N, Beck N, Adalat R, Das S, Glatard T, Evans AC, "CBRAIN: A web based, distributed computing platform for collaborative neuroimaging research", Frontiers in Neuro informatics, Vol 8, Article 54, pp. 1-13,2014.

[58] Shikha Nema, Prof.Shailendra Singh Raghuwanshi," A Novel Approach to Enhanced Security in Public Cloud: Using LDAP Protocol", International Journal of Advanced Research in Computer Engineering & Technology (IJARCET) Volume 3 Issue 9, 2014

[59] Sijin He, Li Guo, Yike Guo, Chao Wu, Moustafa Ghanem, Rui Han, "Elastic Application Container: A Lightweight Approach for Cloud Resource Provisioning", In Proceedings of IEEE International Conference on Advanced Information Networking and Applications (AINA), pp:15 – 22,2012.

[60] Su, Xiaoquan & ma, Yongzheng & Yang, Hongwei & Chang, Xingzhi & Nan, Kai & Xu, Jian & Ning, Kang, "An Open - source Collaboration Environment for Metagenomics Research," In Proceedings of IEEE International Conference on e-Science, pp:7 - 14 ,2011.

[61] Sudha M, Harish G M, Usha J," Performance Analysis of Linux Containers - An Alternative Approach to Virtual Machines", International Journal of Advanced Research in Computer Science and Software Engineering 4(1), IJARCSSE, pp: 820-824 © 2014, January - 2014.

[62] Sveshnikova, Svetlana & Gankevich, Ivan, "Using Virtualisation for Reproducible Research and Code Portability", In Proceedings of International Conference on High Performance Computing & Simulation (HPCS) pp: 891 – 89, 2017.

[63] The NIST Definition of Cloud Computing September 2011.

[64] Thilakanathan D., Chen S., Nepal S., Calvo R.A. "Secure Data Sharing in the Cloud". In: Nepal S., Pathan M. (eds) Security, Privacy and Trust in Cloud Systems. Springer, Berlin, Heidelberg, pp 45-72, 2014.

[65] Thomas F. J. -M. Pasquier, Jatinder Singh, David Eyers, Jean Bacon, "Camflow: Managed Data-Sharing for Cloud Services", IEEE Transactions on Cloud Computing, Volume: 5, Issue: 3, pp: 472 – 484, 2017.

[66] Thomas F. J.-M. Pasquier, Jatinder Singh, Jean Bacon, "Information Flow Control for Strong Protection with Flexible Sharing in PaaS", IEEE International Conference on Cloud Engineering, pp: 279 – 282, 2015.

[67] Thu Yein Win, Fung Po Tso, Quentin Mair, Huaglory Tianfield, "PROTECT: Container Process Isolation Using System Call Interception ", 14th International Symposium on Pervasive Systems, Algorithms and Networks & 2017 11th International Conference on Frontier of Computer Science and Technology & 2017 Third International Symposium of Creative Computing ISPAN-FCST-ISCC), pp: 191-196, 2017.

[68] Thu YeinWin, Fung Po Tso, Quentin Mair, Huaglory Tianfield, "PROTECT: Container Process Isolation Using System Call Interception" 14th International Symposium on Pervasive Systems, Algorithms and Networks & 2017 11th International Conference on Frontier of Computer Science and Technology & Third International Symposium of Creative Computing (ISPAN-FCST-ISCC), pp: 191 – 196, 2017.

[69] Tuan Anh Dinh, Tien & Wenqiang, Wang & Datta, Anwitaman. (2012)." City on the Sky: Extending XACML for Flexible, Secure Data Sharing on the Cloud", Journal of Grid Computing, 10. 10.1007/s10723-012-9212-9.

[70] Uchechukwu Awada ; Adam Barker,"Improving Resource Efficiency of Container-instance Clusters on Clouds", In Proceedings of IEEE/ACM International Symposium on Cluster, Cloud and Grid Computing ,pp. 929-934 , 2017.

[71] Vivek VijaySarkale, Paul Rad, Wonjun Lee, " Secure Cloud Container: Runtime Behavior Monitoring Using Most Privileged Container (MPC)", 2017 IEEE 4thInternational Conference on Cyber Security and Cloud Computing (CSCloud), pp: 351 -356, 2017.

[72] Voss, Alex & Barker, Adam & Asgari-Targhi, Mahboubeh & van Ballegooijen, Adriaan & Sommerville, Ian, "An elastic virtual infrastructure

for research applications (ELVIRA)", Journal of Cloud Computing: Advances, Systems and Applications 2:20, 2013.

[73] Wes Felter, Alexandre Ferreira, Ram Rajamony, Juan Rubio, "An updated performance comparison of virtual machines and Linux containers", 2015 IEEE International Sympo-sium on Performance Analysis of Systems and Software (ISPASS),pp:171 – 172 , 2015.

[74] Xavier, Rafael & Moens, Hendrik & Volckaert, Bruno & De Turck, Filip, (2016) "Adaptive virtual machine allocation algorithms for cloud-hosted elastic media services", pp: 564-570. 10.1109/NOMS.2016.7502859.

[75] Xing Gao, Zhongshu Gu, Mehmet Kayaalp, Dimitrios Pendarakis, Haining Wang, "ContainerLeaks: Emerging Security Threats of Information Leakages in Container Clouds", 2017 47th Annual IEEE/IFIP International Conference on Dependable Systems and Networks (DSN), pp: 237-248, 2017

[76] Xinjie Guan, Xili Wan, Baek-Young Choi, SejunSong, Jiafeng Zhu,"Application Oriented Dynamic Resource Allocation for Data Centers Using Docker Containers", IEEE Communications Letters, Volume: 21, Issue: 3, pp: 504 – 507, 2017.

[77] Y. Chen, P. A. Jamkhedkar, and R. B. Lee, ``A software-hardware architecture for self-protecting data," in Proc. 19th ACM Conf. Comput.Commun. Secur., pp: 14-27, . 2012.

[78] Ye Tao, Xiaodong Wang, Xiaowei Xu, Yinong Chen," Dynamic Resource Allocation Algorithm for Container Based Service Computing", IEEE 13th International Symposium on Autonomous Decentralized System (ISADS), pp: 61 – 67, 2017.

[79] Yongzheng Ma ; Taotao Shi ; Wei Li ; Fang Qian ; Kang Ning ; Chenzhou Cui ; Yunqiang Zhu, "Scientific collaboration cloud platform and its multidisciplinary applications", In Proceedings of IEEE Conference Information Science and Technology (ICIST) , pp.466 – 470 ,2013.

[80] Yujian Zhu ; Junming Ma ; Bo An ; Donggang Cao,"Monitoring and Billing of A Lightweight Cloud System Based on Linux Container" , In Proceedings of International Conference on Distributed Computing Systems Workshops IEEE , pp.325-329,2017.

[81] Zheng Li, Maria Kihl, Qinghua Lu, Jens A. Andersson, "Performance Overhead Comparison between Hypervisor and Container Based Virtualization", IEEE 31st International Conference on Advanced Information Net-working and Applications (AINA), Year: 2017.

[82] "Docker Security". http://docs.docker.com/articles/security.

[83] https://github.com/sagemath

[84] sagemath

PUBLICATIONS

International Journal of Electrical and Computer Engineering (IJECE)
Vol. 8, No. 3, June 2018, pp. 1659~1670
ISSN: 2088-8708, DOI: 10.11591/ijece.v8i3.pp1659-1670

CCCORE: Cloud Container for Collaborative Research

Salini Suresh[1], L. Manjunatha Rao[2]
[1]Computer Science, Bharathiar University, Coimbatore, India
[2]Department of MCA, Dr. Ambedkar Institute of Technology, Bangalore, India

Article Info

Article history:

Received Jun 9, 2017
Revised Jan 1, 2018
Accepted Jan 8, 2018

Keyword:

Cloud computing
Collaborative research
Container
Dynamic allocation
Finish time
Residual resources
Throughput

ABSTRACT

Cloud-based research collaboration platforms render scalable, secure and inventive environments that enabled academic and scientific researchers to share research data, applications and provide access to high- performance computing resources. Dynamic allocation of resources according to the unpredictable needs of applications used by researchers is a key challenge in collaborative research environments. We propose the design of Cloud Container based Collaborative Research (CCCORE) framework to address dynamic resource provisioning according to the variable workload of compute and data-intensive applications or analysis tools used by researchers. Our proposed approach relies on–demand, customized containerization and comprehensive assessment of resource requirements to achieve optimal resource allocation in a dynamic collaborative research environment. We propose algorithms for dynamic resource allocation problem in a collaborative research environment, which aim to minimize finish time, improve throughput and achieve optimal resource utilization by employing the underutilized residual resources.

Corresponding Author:

Salini Suresh,
Computer Science,
Bharathiar University,
Coimbatore, India.
Email: pnsalinisuresh@gmail.com

1. INTRODUCTION

In mid-1990's various grid-based cyberinfrastructures or e-infrastructures were constituted that integrated high-speed research networks and middleware services and endorsed researchers for collaborative sharing of distributed resources. These firmly unified science gateways served as resource providers for specialized as well as generic research initiatives [1]. However, restricted interface to the data, domain-specific nature of science gateways did not match the requirement of the researchers outside those domains [2]. With the advent of cloud computing, easy reconfigurable and adaptive Virtual private research environments and science clouds became a preferred alternative to a traditional grid or cluster-based e-infrastructures. Cloud-based collaborative research platforms provide the researchers with computing, storage resources required to run their applications, and they can collaborate to share data and application, while he concentrates on his area of research. Cloud platform offers compute environment with the huge set of computing resources much bigger than what an individual research organization can afford. Organizations can scale up, scale down the resources, and pay for it according to the usage. Multitenancy provided by cloud architecture enabled the creation of domain and requirement specific virtual private research environments that expedited researchers for collaboration and sharing of the resources [3]. Several science clouds such as Nectar Research cloud [4] provides the infrastructure to run compute-intensive scientific applications [5], [6]. Even though a substantial amount of research work has been carried out with regard to cloud-based collaborative research platforms, ample work does not exist in view of dynamic resource allocation in collaborative research cloud frameworks.

A Container based Collaborative Research Cloud framework with a hybrid access control approach for enhanced isolation

Salini Suresh
Department of Computer science
Seshadripuram Academy of Business Studies
Bangalore
pnsalinisuresg@gmail.com

L. Manjunatha Rao
Department of MCA
Dr. Ambedkar Institute of Technology
Bangalore
manjuarjun2004@yahoo.com

Abstract--**Secure sharing of sensitive research data and tools over a public network like internet is an arduous challenge for the researchers. The fundamental aim of the research is to design a Collaborative Research Cloud (CRC) framework grounded on cloud to expedite collaborative research where researchers can emulate the shared tools and inferences to run independently in a secured, contained environment. We have applied a hybrid access control model, which authenticates, authorises the researchers for secure sharing of resources in a heterogeneous cloud environment. CRC achieves faster resource allocation using custom-built containers. Further, we put forward an optimal resource allocation algorithm based on containerization. We evaluated CRC for resource allocation and container isolation. The proposed access control model enhances** the **resource allocation and isolation in CRC**.

Keywords--Collaborative Research, Container, Isolation, Resource allocation, Access control

I. INTRODUCTION

A collaborative research framework build on a cloud should enable researchers in diverse organisations and purviews to work concurrently and share data and tools whilst providing isolation for the researcher's data and applications [1]. However, heterogeneous tools, inferences and computing platforms used by researcher poses a challenge in design of collaborative research framework.

A collaborative research cloud framework pertaining to cloud should enable the researchers to simulate the research environment independent of the platform. The multi-tenant architecture offered by cloud endows the creation of virtual private research environments for the researchers to collaborate [2].Researchers need to share raw data, specific tool or an inference basedon his research imperatives. In our collaborative research cloud (CRC) framework, each authenticated researcher is granted custom-built containers consisting of heterogeneous tools, inferences, data that can run independent of the platform.

Even though various file hosting and cloud content management services are available, it is unviable to use these services for huge volumes of research data. The proposed CRC framework is not dependent on any public, paid file services hosting instead it relies on containerisation for sharing of sensitive research data and resources in collaborative environment [3].

Necessity might often arise for the researchers to make multiple environments, which can generate different inferences based on the parameters [4]. A heterogeneous collaborative research framework should connect researchers from different organisations and enable them to select a specific tool available anywhere and analyse the data available in any repository [5]. The novel feature of the proposed CRC is that it allows researchers to collaborate and work on an existing project by duplicating the same parameters irrespective of the local host environment. The Research Owner (RO) packages container with any set of data, parameters, and inferences based on those parameters, tools with all its dependencies and allocates it to any authorized researcher (R_n) who request for it. The requested resources allocation can be achieved faster using containerization [6].Even though containers accelerates resourceallocation,it lacks in extent of isolation provided to researcher's data and application [7].

Strong authentication mechanisms and access control rules can address numerous security issues, which arises due to lack of trust mechanisms or multitenancy[8][9]. In our CRC framework, users from multiple independent clouds are authenticated based on credentials and characteristics .A preeminent solution for this is to deploy an external centralized authentication using LDAP, which is a platform independent external authentication protocol to improve security and efficiency of CRC [10]. A collaborative research framework should enable the resource sharing and protect the user's resources from unauthorised access [11]. The secured and granular access control model deployed in CRC binds

978-1-5386-2361-9/17/$31.00 ©2017 IEEE

International Journal of Computing Science and Information Technology, **2018**,
ISSN: 2278-9669, April 2018 (http://ijcsit.org)

A Methodical Review Of Virtualization Techniques In Cloud Computing

Salini Suresh [1].
Seshadripuram Academy of Business Studies,
Bangalore, India;

Manjunatha Rao [2].
Dr. Ambedkar Institute of Technology,
Bangalore, India,

Received January 2018

Abstract

IT enterprises has widely embraced virtualization trend to incorporate autonomic computing. Server virtualization empowers the creation of virtual environments that are adept to run operating system and applications. Recent IDC survey forecasts that companies can achieve a return of investment of 472 percent by utilizing virtualization. We have presented a detailed overview of Hypervisor based and container based implementations. We reviewed the existing approaches of performance evaluation and analysis of the virtualisation tools.

Keywords: Virtualization, Hypervisor, VM, Container

I. Introduction

Virtualization can be defined as "framework or methodology of dividing the resources of a computer into multiple implementation environments, by concerning one or more notions or technologies such as software partitioning, hardware division, time-sharing, partial or complete machine simulation, emulation, worth of service, and many others"[1]. Server virtualization facilitates the creation of several isolated virtual instances from one physical server. Virtualization conceals the identity of server resources from server users and each virtual server will performance like a physical server. Network virtualization pools the accessible assets of a system to the available bandwidth into independent channels that can be allocated to a particular server. Storage virtualization merge physical storage from many devices to a single storage pool.

Cloud implementation benefits largely by virtualization as it allows the creation of virtual instances of physical resources [2]. The core paybacks of virtualization are hardware independence, multitenancy, flexibility, increased isolation, and enhanced security. The virtualization systems are categorized into are full virtualization, Para virtualization, and operating system level virtualization. In Full virtualization operating systems and applications are isolated from the computer hardware by a software called Hypervisor thus provides each Virtual machine (VM) a complete abstraction VMware [3] and KVM [4] uses this type of hardware virtualization. Xen [3] uses Para virtualization where hypervisor changes the guest in an operating system in contrast to virtual machine model, which allows a guest operating system to run without modifications. Operating System Level virtualization or container-based virtualization creates user instances or containers isolated from each other. Linux-VServer [5], OpenVZ [6] and Linux Containers (LXC) [7]) practices container-based virtualization, which is lightweight compared to VM based model. The rest of the manuscript is organised as follows: Section II describes background and related work.

Section III discusses an overview of virtualisation techniques. In Section IV performance analysis of virtualisation techniques is in existing approaches are reviewed.

II. BACK GROUND AND RELATED WORK

Most of the common server operating systems lack configuration isolation, which requires the installation of a separate instance of the operating system for each application in a virtual machine. Virtualization techniques should provide the resource isolation in a cloud framework [8]. Hypervisor-based systems are the most accepted solution for cloud virtualization [9].Bare metal hypervisor or Type-1 Hypervisors can be mounted on the hardware directly whereas hosted hypervisor or Type-2 hypervisor entails a host operating system. Kernel Virtual Machine (KVM) is a virtualization tool for Linux [10].

ijecs open access www.ijecs.in
International Journal Of Engineering And Computer Science ISSN:2319-7242
Volume – 5 Issue -03 March, 2016 Page No. 16047-16049

Analysis of Security threats in ad hoc cloud.

[1]Mrs. Salini Suresh, [2]Dr.L.Manjunath Rao

[1]Research scholar Bharathiar University, Coimbotore.
151,12th cross, 5th main NGEF layout, Nagarbhavi, Bangalore, 9663363201
pnsalinisuresh@gmail.com
[2]Head, MCA department, Dr. Ambedkar Institute of Technology, Bangalore,
manjuarjun2004@yahoo.com

Abstract

The cloud is redefining the IT architectures of various business domains. Organizations have clearly recognized the unlimited benefits of cloud like dynamic payloads on the technical side and elastic financial models on the commercial side which guarantees in greater than before efficiency. The benefits of cloud computing can be maximized fully by applying novel technologies in security and risk management processes. The risk factors in terms of security is much more in public cloud computing compared to traditional computing which are bases on datacenter . In a highly shared ad hoc cloud environment which is in the control of instance-to-instance network connectivity security of the applications and sensitive data is a big challenge faced by the cloud providers. As the entire stack of applications, platform, infrastructure of the cloud is designed and managed by service providers the cloud users are uncertain about the security. This paper studies the generic security challenges in an ad hoc cloud environment .the security challenges and mitigations are discussed in section I. A survey was conducted with users of cloud from domains like health care, education and retail business. Analysis of survey data and the results are also discussed in section II.

Introduction

Ad hoc clouds rely on scalable virtualization technology which gives its user access to set of non-dedicated computing resources. The users of an ad hoc cloud are in a highly shared environment where resources are dynamically provisioned and organizations share the same remotely located physical hardware with strangers. Security and privacy has been the biggest challenges for organizations who are already using cloud as end to end solution for their IT needs and who are still considering moving into cloud. In a SPI model of cloud SaaS demands security at all levels of user identity and data access and maintain integrity and continuity of the applications. In IaaS secure networking and trusted computing should be the prime concern, and whereas at PaaS demands protection at the resource-management level.[1]

Section I
Security challenges in Ad hoc cloud model.

1) *Identity and Access Management (IAM)*: The service provider in responsible for security of applications and users have less control over the security. In an ad hoc cloud environment where highly mobile users and multiple end devices, identity and access management is a key issue. IAM has to be addressed by proactive and reactive security tools .Implementing a strong IAM can be done through protocols like security assertion markup language (SAML) [2].

2) *Data leakage and protection* : sensitive organizational data is stored as plain text in cloud environments are more prone to breaches. Secure data processing and storage is usually the responsibility the service provider [3].Data protection can be achieved giving the access rights to the users at multiple levels. Encryption is an effective way to provide the control over their confidential data. Users have exclusive control of the encryption keys, and therefore control of their own data with in their environment[4] .There are no clear standards on how to the cloud service provider should do a recycling of storage resources like memory or disk space. When these resources are not properly recycled there are high chances of data remanence . Solution for data remanence can be established through service level agreements which should clearly state the strategies for data deletion once a tenant vacates the storage space [5].

The other persistent threats faced in ad hoc cloud environment can be:

3) *Hypervisor attacks*: In a multitenant ad hoc cloud users highly share physical resources with others through common software virtualization layers. With an added risk to user's resource stack, the cloud user consumer is completely ignorant of another tenants identity and intentions. The virtual machine could be malicious and prone to hypervisor attacks or sniff communications. Vulnerability of side-channel attack in a cloud environment where a virtual machine sharing the same resource induce a arbitrary code into another virtual machine [6]. using TCCP (trusted cloud computing platform) secured Infrastructure as a service

DOI: http://dx.doi.org/10.26483/ijarcs.v9i2.5733

ISSN No. 0976-5697

Volume 9, No. 2, March-April 2018

International Journal of Advanced Research in Computer Science

RESEARCH PAPER

Available Online at www.ijarcs.info

AN APPROACH TO IMPROVE ISOLATION AND SECURITY IN CONTAINER BASED CLOUD SYSTEMS.

Salini Suresh
Department of Computer science
Seshadripuram Academy of Business Studies
Bangalore, India

Manjunatha Rao
Department of MCA
Dr. Ambedkar Institute of Technology
Bangalore, India

Abstract: Container-based virtualization is a lightweight virtual hosting environment that provides application isolation with less overhead. Containerization enables the creation of isolated, multiple user-space instances and effectual consumption of resources and rapid provisioning. However, container-based virtual environments have a weak isolation due to a shared kernel. This makes the entire system vulnerable to security attacks. This paper investigates various security issues in container based systems and proposes a solution for securing the container using a novel access control model. We also conducted stress test using benchmarking tool to evaluate the enhanced isolation using our proposed model.

Keywords: cloud, container, security, isolation, authorisation, access control.

I. INTRODUCTION

Virtualization enables resource sharing using emulation of resources. The hypervisor-based virtualization provides sufficient isolation between guest virtual machines but imposes significant overheads. On the other hand, in container-based virtualization, the host operating system is virtualized to aid multiple guest containers run on top of host operating system without installing the added kernel for the guest containers, which substantially reduces the performance overhead [1].

Kernel namespaces and control groups are deployed to realize isolation between guests and host operating system in Linux kernels. Namespaces offer resource isolation, network isolation while cgroups bring about the resources, process control and depict the configuration of a network. The multiple processes added to cgroup shares all the resources allocated to that group [2]. LXC has also taken on of Linux Kernel features like chroot, Process identifier (PID) and permit users to build and manage applications using APIs.

Even though namespaces and Linux kernel feature perk up container security, there exist various security issues due to a shared kernel and weak isolation. In this paper, we investigate the security risks associated with a container based virtual environment.

The major contributions of this paper are the following:

- We identify the security concerns in container based virtual environments.
- We review the mechanisms to mitigate the identified security issues.
- Propose a model to enhance the isolation and security of the cloud container-based environment.
- Benchmarking the proposed model and evaluate the performance.

The rest of the paper is organized as follows:

In Section II we have discussed security concerns in cloud container based environments. Section III details the existing security mechanisms that are deployed to address the challenges in container security. Section IV explains the proposed approach. Section V explains the access control process flow of the security module. In section VI evaluation of proposed system and the results are discussed.

II. SECURITY VULNERABILITIES

Containers suffer from weak isolation owing to sharing of the system kernel. Any malicious code can get proliferated to other containers and underlying operating system. A malicious container on the host can compromise the security of other containers and thus the entire system.

A user with root privileges on the container can mount and access any directory from the host even the root directory [3] which exposes the host to a threat called root breakout. A process that breaks out of the guest container has same access privileges on the host including root privileges. Host break in attack turns out on the allocated container when the host root gains access to containers and modifies it [4]. A user with uid 0 will be root on the host with full root access privileges on the host. This can lead to privilege escalation attacks where a user gets privileges like root users.

The multi-tenant container cloud-based systems where multiple containers share the host resources are vulnerable to threats like information leakage [5]. Adversaries can take advantage of these information leakage channels and instigate attack that affects the confidentiality and integrity of the entire system [6].

The container daemon is easily accessible from a web interface which makes the applications in the container it prone to security attacks. Malicious applications in the container to tire out the system resources to an extent those other applications are unable to use them, like in the case of threats like Denial of service (DOS) [7]. Container lacks an additional layer of isolation provided by the hypervisor which makes it effortless for attackers to launch into the host machine. Cloud container based environments that lack strong access control policies are susceptible to cross site scripting [8] attacks that let the attacker instill client side script into web pages.

www.ingramcontent.com/pod-product-compliance
Lightning Source LLC
LaVergne TN
LVHW082350200926
848481LV00012B/3518